A MIND FOR LIFE

Live your truth by choosing how you think and feel

NATHAN WALLACE

Emery Lincoln Publishing

A MIND FOR LIFE

Live your truth by choosing how you think and feel

Emery Lincoln Publishing is owned by Nathan Wallace

www.emerylincoln.com

In memory of my father

Emery Wallace

For my Mother and my Sister

Contents

Preface

This book is for anyone who wants to make a change for the better in their life. Although written towards the individual, this information is also for any group, however large or small, that wants to grow and prosper. If you as an individual or group are in a place of stagnation, and want to know how to get out of that place... read this book.

A Mind for Life presents the idea that you have the ability to choose your life –every detail. You will see that 'life' –its situations, people, things, etc., are *not* things that just happen randomly, but are chosen by **YOU** in every aspect. You will also be given ways on *how to* ignite your very own personal transformation. This transformation will empower you as *the* one who deliberately creates your own life story!

Within these pages is contained powerful, life changing wisdom. Just reading *A Mind for Life* will cause an opening and shift within you... that's how impactful this knowledge is. Your health, your finances, your relationships, your work...your *mind...* will never be the same.

<u>I will show you how this works</u> by using the concept of **Perspective**. I will also give you real-time 'techniques' that will allow you to purposefully deepen and extend your growth; within the day-to-day life that you are already living.

Having *A Mind for Life* means that you not only desire the best for yourself, your relationships, your health, your finances, and the Earth, but it also means that you realize that you have the ability to choose the best in all of these areas... *and* bring it forth. This way of seeing yourself and doing things becomes your mindset and way of life. You *do not* have to blindly believe in the contents of this book. You only have to be open minded enough to consider its contents objectively...and you *will* be transformed. This book links the doing with the understanding of the doing. You will know *what* to do and *why* you are doing it.

From the joy that you have to the depression that you may feel...from the person that you bumped into on the street, to your soul mate ...from the vitality and strength in your body to an ache, pain or disease that you may have...*you* and only *you* are the author –not environment, people, genetics, good or bad luck -but *you* and only *you*.

Right now, you're probably asking...how??? "How am I doing all of this? Are you saying I've given myself this bad romance? This illness? This low paying salary? This addiction? All of this drama? It makes no sense - why would I do that to myself??? I only want the best for myself"!

The answer is once again –yes...**_YOU_** are doing all of it! And the answer to *how* you're doing it, is by your *perspective* - - -that is... how you see or *behold* things. Yes, it's that simple, the root or foundation of everything you are creating and thus experiencing in your life is from your *perspective*.

What I'm going to show you is something (perspective) that *is* working already and always *has been* working. The ability to choose your life through *perspective* is part of your nature; it is <u>not</u> a gift or ability that is 'out there' somewhere.

This book will serve to increase your awareness of this part of yourself that has been, up until now, 'behind the scenes'…'pulling the strings'. This is a very practical, hands-on awareness, and day by day you will become more conscious of this choosing that you are doing. You will find yourself making more deliberate, conscious choices in <u>every</u> aspect of your daily life. This will lead to your discovery of a new level of freedom, self-empowerment and joy!

Nathan Wallace
Chicago/New York
February 2016

Chapter 1

Perspective

When is the last time you faced reality? If I call you a dreamer, living in your own world, would that bother you? This is something I'm sure most of us have been asked before. The people, who asked us these types of questions, assumed they knew what life was all about. After all, everyone in their house and neighborhood was asking us the same questions! They had agreement among themselves as to what the outer world and reality was all about. It seemed almost futile and a hopeless cause for us to disagree with *all* of them. It felt overwhelming; but yet somewhere deep inside, we knew there was something more. Since then, we went on in life, some of us accepting their views and some of us didn't. Now we all have come together, here at this point in time; so let's begin to pull back the layers and get to that 'something more' that we always knew was there.

We need to start off by going into this idea of *Perspective* and getting clarity on what it is and its importance. Perspective, simply put, is how you see something. At a basic level, this is what you are experiencing when you look out at something in the physical world. For example, if two people are both looking at a chair, they really are not looking at the same thing. First of all, they are at entirely different angles to the chair, that is, one person may be to the right and the other person may be more to the left, if even slightly. So both people are actually looking at two different parts of the chair... they are seeing different things. I can illustrate this to you by asking you to hold up your hand, what do you see? Do you see the whole hand? The

1

answer is no, you are seeing it from a certain perspective. Now if you hold your hand in front of a mirror, you would see your hand from an entirely different view... in the mirror, that same hand will look different to you.

How many of us, have seen our whole hand at once?

The above illustration gives you a very simplistic example of basic perspective. Oftentimes, we assume we have the whole perspective on something but we really only have a part of it. How many of us, have seen our whole hand at once? That can sound like a funny question, but it does allow me to take you a little deeper into this understanding of perspective. Consider again the two people looking at the chair, one person has 20/20 vision whereas the other is farsighted... do you think they are *experiencing* the chair in exactly the same way? The person with 20/20 vision is able to see the details of the craftsmanship of the chair with much more clarity than the person who is farsighted. This may cause the person who has the 20/20 vision to appreciate the chair's beauty more, like it and maybe even buy that chair. Whereas the person with far-sighted vision, to them, it just looks like a plain chair.

The above example serves to give us even more clarity on the nature of perspective. Now we are seeing how perspective goes from just being a purely physical act of perception, to having something to do with our *experiencing* something. What's important here is that perspective goes far beyond sense perception to include ones *mental view* of facts, ideas and the relationships between them. In the example above, the far-sighted person, because of their inability to perceive the fine details in the craftsmanship of the chair, didn't have the same *experience* of the chair as the person with 20/20 vision; and their(the far-sighted person) tastes were not stimulated enough for them to want to buy that chair.

That being said, when we say *perspective* is how you see something, in addition to the physical act of perception, we are also talking about a mental view ,an attitude, the way in which we regard some situation, person, place or thing.

A mental view is always bundled with a purely physical perception. That is, we don't just see a person, place, thing or event with our physical eyes; we also have within us a "notion" or *mental* view of whatever we perceive. This mental view is intimately intertwined with our perception; and sometimes we're more conscious of this mental view, and sometimes we're not. *Consciousness* is the keyword here. Consciousness, or in other words...*awareness* of whatever mental view or attitude we have about what we perceive. This awareness, of whatever mental view/attitude we hold when we perceive something, is more or less present to us. What I'm saying will be made instantly clear to you by a simple example. Let's say you plug a device of yours into an outlet...it could be a hairdryer, for example. The hairdryer is plugged in and working fine, then, all of the sudden, sparks fly everywhere and the plug and outlet catch on fire! What do you see? What do you do? Of course you see that your outlet and socket is on fire...that is simple enough. That is your immediate perception of the event...you see the fire, you smell the smoke, and you may have heard a pop as well.

This is just the purely physical aspect of your perspective. And we call this perception; and your *perspective* does include this perception component. You see, hear, taste, touch or smell something. On this aspect of perspective, we are grounded in the 5 senses. And this is equally valid across all of your senses. Your perception is the first phase of your perspective on something. The music producer *hears* the music first and foremost. The chef *tastes* and *smells* the food. The painter *sees* the colors on the palate. The carpenter runs their hand across the wood to *feel* its roughness or smoothness. When we are in a perspective on something, we often take this perception aspect for granted. Unless there is an issue, our 5 senses are running in the background...they are a given.

Perspective includes a mental view or notion about what we perceive.

Now, using our exploding hair dryer example let's move on to the second aspect of perspective... having a mental view, attitude or notion about what we perceive. Remember, that having a perspective on something includes much more than just the physical act of touching it, tasting it, seeing it, smelling it or hearing it. Perspective includes a mental view or notion about what we perceive.

In our example, you saw the hairdryer's socket on fire along with the outlet. This was something you *saw*...something that was perceived. But you didn't just stop there. You snatched the cord out of the wall and grabbed a *dry* towel to smother the little fire that was starting. Why did you do all of this? Was it because of what you saw? Yes and No.

Yes... in that of course...you *saw* a fire and you put it out before it got out of control, that much is obvious...right? In other words, if there was no fire, there would be nothing to put out...and how did you know there was a fire starting? Because you saw it. Again, in this sense, the answer is yes...you put the fire out because you *saw* it. This is that first stage of perspective that we have been talking about, we call it *perception*. I am, however going to tell you that you did not put out the fire because you saw it. Sure, seeing the fire did play a role, but you didn't put out the fire because you saw it.

This may not seem so obvious at first, but it's true. Again, going back to our example of the burning hairdryer, you did not, put out the fire that it started because you saw the outlet and the hairdryer's cord on fire...no. You put out the fire because you knew if you didn't, the whole house would burn down! You had an understanding of what could happen if this fire was not put out...you had a mental view or notion. Your mental view included what fire does when it's not contained; of what fire can do to houses...wood, paper, plastic, etc. And what it can do to the people, pets and other possessions of the house. You knew of how a fire can spread to other houses in the neighborhood and even the town. So in the blink of an eye...*without thinking*, you reached over and squashed the fire!

Now I'm saying that you didn't just put out the fire because you saw fire. No, you put it out because you had a mental view of things in that moment. The perception of "fire" is not enough to impel you to put it out. A few years ago, a friend and I were looking for a new place to have dinner at...we wanted to eat somewhere that was different and a little exciting. We drove around for about a half-hour until we came upon a Hitachi Grill style restaurant; where they cook with an open flame. In this particular restaurant, there was a huge grill in the middle of the whole restaurant. And there seemed to be crowds of people gathered around the grill waiting for their food and watching the chef do their magic. The chef used an open flame on the grill...I mean real huge flames shoot off the grill about 2 feet into the air...amazing! The chef would flip and sling the food, using the spatula, up into the air from off the grill...the flames meeting the food in the air. The chef would continue these acrobatics until the food was done. The food was great, and everyone had a good time.

5

In this case, 'fire' was a good thing...it helped to create great food and an enjoyable experience. The fire was part of the cooking experience and of the fun of eating at this particular restaurant. I never became afraid that the flame would get out of control or become a bad thing. And the flames were nearly 2 feet high off the grill! Although I was perceiving 'fire', I had a different mindset or mental view from what I would have in the case of the exploding hairdryer. Remember that *mental view* is the way in which we regard some person, place, thing or situation. At this grill, I knew the cook had skill, the grill was made of iron; this was a style of cooking that had been perfected over probably centuries. I also knew the restaurant had fire extinguishers, etc., etc. All of these things that I knew in the background of my mind's eye constituted my underlying *mental view* of 'fire' in that context, which allowed me to have a different experience from the hairdryer example.

So let's summarize what we have so far:

Perspective is defined as how you see something.

Perspective has 2 aspects or phases:

1). Perception which is defined as *the physical act of sensing something*; it could be a person, place, thing, situation, event or whatever. Your eyes see the tree in front of you. Your ears hear the wind blowing and so on for the rest of your senses.

2). Mental view/Attitude which is defined as the way in which we regard a person, place, thing, situation, event or whatever. Your eyes see the tree in front of you not only as 'tree', but the tree is beautiful. You have an inner attitude or view point on what you are sensing. That is, you see that the 'fire' burning in your fire place is the same 'fire' that's burning up your hairdryer cord, but your mental view or attitude is quite different with regards to each event where the 'fire' is burning...'fire' burning in the fire place is nice, it keeps you warm and adds to the atmosphere. Whereas 'fire' burning up your hairdryer cord, is a dangerous thing and must be put out immediately.

So now that we have these 2 aspects of perspective understood, I want to move on into the third and final aspect of perspective. This third aspect of perspective is what I like to call **Impression**.

Impression is when the mental view/attitude is placed *onto* what you are sensing (onto the perception). So think of it like this, there is the person, place, thing or situation that is there in the outer world, your five senses pick it up...we know that as perceiving or the *perception*. Ok, now in addition to the raw perception, there is the underlying mental view or attitude about what you are perceiving..."that fire is dangerous", "she looks angry", etc. Now the *Impression* comes in when our *mental view/attitude is* placed upon our perception in such a way as to make whatever we perceive in the outer world <u>match</u> our inner *mental view/attitude* about it.

Impression is how we clothe our outer world with flesh and blood...with meaning.

A chair is just a chair... nothing more, nothing less. However, when we see the chair, it doesn't just end there; we bring our mental view to that experience. The mental view we bring is impressed up the 'chair', now the chair has meaning for us. That is, the chair is now beautiful, comfortable, a keepsake, etc. Impression is how we clothe our outer world with flesh and blood...with meaning. It would be a very detached, robotic and

7

alienated existence if we just lived purely by perception only; and being feeling, thinking, colorful, vibrant beings, we cannot.

Impression, allows us to go from a flat 2-D experience of what we perceive, to a fleshed-out, 3-D experience with color and meaning. Artists do this all the time when they use the skill of perspective. Perspective as used in the artistic realm is, in principle, the same thing as when it's occurs naturally in relation to Impression, in our everyday lives. In Art, when an artist uses the technique of perspective, they impress a 3-D representation onto a flat 2-D surface. The Artist is putting their inner vision of something that has height, width *and* depth onto a flat piece of paper or canvas which has only height and width. What the Artist has put out there can look very real, but it's just an illusion.

The Artist has painted a picture of a beautiful country road scene. We see a tree-lined, winding road that recedes into the 'distance'; the trees getting smaller and darker as they go 'away' from us. There are rugged, snowcapped mountains in the 'distance' embraced by gentle clouds and little specks that appear to be birds flying. A scene like this can appear very life-like; and draw us into its atmosphere... its world. We can even get lost in emotion over such a scene, the scene however, is an illusion. The canvas is still actually flat...2-D. Through the Artist's use of the skill of perspective, they have pulled us into another world. The Artist has *impressed* upon the outer (the canvas), their inner *mental view* of mountains, trees, clouds, etc. In effect this has created a reality unto itself, namely the beautiful work of art that we see.

Life becomes our very own work of art. We paint our own picture in life. We give what we perceive in the outer world, its meaning when we place or impress our mental views and attitudes on them. Two people look at a glass of water, one person says the glass is half empty, the other person says it's half full. Both are seeing the same glass, with the same water in it, but the both are having a different experience of what they perceive because of their different mind sets.

So now let's put it all together:

Perspective is defined as how you see something.

Perspective has 3 aspects or phases:

1). Perception which is defined as *the physical act of sensing something*; it could be a person, place, thing, situation, event or whatever. Your eyes see the tree in front of you. Your ears hear the wind blowing and so on for the rest of your senses. This, in our context, is pretty straight forward.

2). Mental view/Attitude which is defined as the way in which we regard a person, place, thing, situation, event or whatever. Your eyes see the tree in front of you not only as 'tree', but the tree is beautiful. You have an inner attitude or view point on what you are sensing. That is, you see that the 'fire' burning in your fire place is the same 'fire' that's burning up your hairdryer cord, but your mental view or attitude is quite different with regards to each event where the 'fire' is burning. In other words, 'fire' burning in the fire place is nice; it keeps you warm and adds mood to the atmosphere. Whereas 'fire' burning up your hairdryer cord, is a dangerous thing and must be squashed right away.

3). Impression which is defined as placing a mental view/attitude upon what is perceived. The tree that we perceive is beautiful and not just a 'tree' because we have placed our inner attitudes and concepts of beauty upon what we perceive…the tree. This impressing that we do, not only gives relational and aesthetic significance to our lives, but it also is an essential survival mechanism as well. The fire in the fireplace is great; it keeps you warm and can add a sense of atmosphere to the room. Whereas the fire burning up your hairdryer is no good and must be put out before it causes more damage.

Now that we have our concept of **Perspective** nicely laid out, how does this fit in with you choosing and transforming your life for the better? There are situations in all of our lives that we would like to have full say-so over; some of us want to live with more joy, some better health, others more efficiency on their jobs in the work place, still others desire to just be present in every moment of their lives, noticing the gifts and beauty of Nature and the world around them. While there are many different ways to get to these states of being, I will tell you that an understanding of **Perspective**, as presented in this book, is one of the simplest ways to get to where you want to be. One of, if not the greatest, powers you have is your natural ability to *behold*…to have **Perspective**! And yet a vast majority of us are living apparently random lives. We get into seemingly random personal relationships that either brings us pain or that don't enhance who we are. We get into mediocre jobs, making mediocre money and can't pay the bills…the list goes on and on.

I am here to tell you that you *can* choose your life; that personal transformation is real. Now that we have a good, basic understanding of what **Perspective** is, let's dive a little deeper and see *how* we use it. In order to have a mind for life and choose something better, we need to know *how* we are doing the choosing. In fact, many of us are not *aware* that we are even doing the choosing...but we are... every bit of it! Have you ever heard the statement..."Life happens"? I'm sure many of us have, and I'm here to tell you...nothing could be further from the truth!

<u>Principles</u>

1). *Perspective*, at a very basic level, is how you see something.

2). We learned that Perspective includes *Perception*, which is the physical act of having awareness through the five senses.

3). Perspective also includes a *mental view or attitude*.

4). *Impression* is the act of us placing our perspective on what we perceive.

5). Impression gives meaning.

6). Our perspectives can go unaware to us unless we are conscious.

7). One of the greatest powers we have is our ability to have Perspective...to be able to behold.

Chapter 2

Mindfulness and State of Being

Did you know you are choosing your life? Well... you are. When I say this to people, I tend to get a mixture of reactions. But in general, the responses tend to come in two opposite sides. On the one hand, people have an instant inner recognition, and shall I dare to say *remembrance*, of this as true; and they begin to piece together their lives and understand why things have been going the way they have. On the other hand, some people tend to lash back out at me and accuse me of being unrealistic; and of me even being unfair because the bad things that 'happened' to them were done by someone else, or 'the system' or they just 'happened'. Maybe this second group is not ready for the responsibility of this truth, but whether they are ready or not, they are still choosing their lives and all of its twists and turns, peaks and valleys.

So, as I began to think about the naysayers, I realized that it wasn't so much about them having unbelief in what I was saying that was the real problem... not at all; I mean, who wouldn't like to be able to create their lives 'to order'...right? There is something very important I must point out here: choosing your life is not about it being drama-free or only about sweet and good things happening....in fact the opposite is often true. It's from the unwanted, the mistakes and the drama that we often learn and grow. So it occurred to me that the people who did not believe in what I was saying, would still really love to have this empowerment, if only they could see it, if only they could become conscious, and become aware that it was *already* going on within them. All they had to do was direct it. It was at this point, that I began to understand what ***Mindfulness*** could mean to everyone.

Mindfulness

Mindfulness is a 'place' within you; it is a place of nothingness and at the same time of the infinite. In its own right, it is a state of quietness, stillness, peace and infinite potential power. It is an infinite, blank slate of all possibility existing outside of time and not bound by its rules. It is beyond the scope of this book to teach about how to achieve Mindfulness, that is an entire field unto itself. However, I will share with you an experience of mine that may shed some light.

A few years ago, I had a more than normal inner desire to grow more spiritually and in my life as a whole. Praying was one of my main ways of creating change within me. I had never really meditated, and my concept of it was really inaccurate. I thought it meant me living isolated from the world like a monk or something. Doing a bunch of rituals and chants that were strange and weird to me; up until then I just couldn't relate to it based on my ideas about it.

I began to understand meditation as any process or activity that brought me into a quiet mind...

But as I looked into personal growth and development ideas further, the concept of meditation began to simplify to me. I began to understand it as doing something to attain a quiet mind. And the 'something' that I needed to do could be many things! I didn't have to dress in long robes, burn candles and go off into the mountains...no. I began to understand meditation as any process or activity that brought me into a quiet mind, where an inner peace and clarity were. So a person could be praying and meditating, riding their bike and meditating, cooking and meditating, making music and meditating, etc.; etc. It really was simpler than I had thought. We often don't realize how busy our minds can get. With the vast amount of information that is available to us today through the internet and media, many people are just over stimulated with thought. The mind is constantly 'chattering' and analyzing; even replaying pieces of songs, conversations and scenarios over and over within our heads. It can be very tiring. Some of us have never experienced what the inner peace of having a quiet mind is like; I really didn't either until that time.

It was with that quiet mind that I began to experience something else within myself. As I progressed, I found the best and most complete way for me to meditate was just to relax in a quiet room, alone, with my cell phone and other things like the television, computers, etc., turned off. For the first time, it seemed, I was alone with myself. In a strange way it was like I was connecting with my core, real self again.

I had, unknowingly over time, totally identified myself with my mind.

When I would begin to relax my mind, it would be moving at what seemed to be faster that the speed of light. It would be calculating what I needed to do later that day, what I did the day before; it would be figuring out what 'this' meant, what 'that' meant; it would figuring out and recycling so many things at once, and it was on automatic with this. It seemed like I had no control and I couldn't stop the constant 'chatter'. My mind was pushy and stubborn, and I had, unknowingly over time, totally identified myself with my mind. It was like a mad house!

15

No clarity, no peace! It was the very act of trying to meditate that showed me all of this. Before, this constant 'chatter' was the norm; I really didn't realize there was something else...I had nothing to compare it to. The restless mind was me; I had unknowingly identified myself with it.

So as I allowed myself to relax, after many days, that mental restlessness, and even thought as I knew it, would slip away every once in a while. It was at these moments that I would experience this Mindfulness that I've been telling you about. It felt like a vast outer space that was infinitely aware of every-thing. It felt like it had no beginning and that it was all things; and was the potential of all things that existed or that could emerge into being. It was outside of time. It was an inner peace and infinite power at the same time. I didn't have a name for this at the time, but I was experiencing Mindfulness.

...we are dealing with a revealed type of knowing, rather than an analytical one...

Please don't try and analyze this description I'm giving you. Something like this is not of the realm of spoken language; this type of thing is *revealed* to you, you don't have to figure it out or understand it. This is because, the mind that analyzes and 'understands' is the very thing that we are allowing to fall away when we meditate; this mind is not designed to 'understand' *this*, in fact we want this mind out of the way when we medi-tate. Maybe in another book I will lay out for you the different types of knowing. Here, with regards to meditation, we are dealing with a revealed type of knowing, rather than an analytical one; both of these types of knowing are important, and equally valid, they just play different roles for different purposes. So, it is only when the mind quiets down and stops all the analyzing that a person can know about this.

After some time, I began to learn how to allow myself to relax more and more and therefore, I was experiencing this Mindfulness more often. Eventually, something interesting started to happen. When I would be out on my normal daily activities, and even interacting with other people, I began to notice myself as an awareness that was observing me and everything else. This awareness was like a big *inner eye*. I began to be aware of my inner thoughts, intuitions, emotions and body states before they would happen...and also while they were happening...in real-time!

So what does this all have to do with you choosing and having a mind for life? The answer is everything. **Mindfulness** didn't just make me aware in some detached, non-emotional way of my life. I became aware that I was *not* my thoughts, emotions or body. I got in touch with something much bigger and more infinite. What it did do, was put me in touch with a **broader perspective**. This *broader perspective* wasn't just limited to my thoughts, feelings or body state; but included all possibility! And that is the key here.

Broader Perspective-The Big Eye

The **broader perspective** that Mindfulness brings you to, is not a particular thought or *mental view* you may have. Mindfulness's *broader perspective* is <u>all</u> choice, <u>all</u> possibility...not just your localized point of view. And what is crucial also, is that it brings you an overarching, intuitive awareness that you are indeed choosing and that you have a perspective. This **broader perspective** brings you into an awareness of your inner state. That is, your inner thoughts, feelings and how your body feels to you. You are aware of this as if you are looking at yourself having these thoughts, feelings and body states from above. It's like having a big, quiet, infinite eye within you that <u>is</u> you but is detached and watching from a 'distance'. This *big inner eye* is seeing everything that's happening with you take place in something like slow-motion. This big inner eye is an observer that never sleeps and does not judge. This big eye is always in the present, and shall I say... an infinite present. It is a very calm, quiet, all 'seeing-ness' within you; that is everything and at the same time, is nothing at all. This big eye is much like the nature of Mindfulness itself; which dwells in the ever- present moment of Now.

The **broader perspective** allows you to become aware that you are coming out of a given state of being, and that you do indeed have a perspective on something. The inner knowingness of the nature of a perspective that you may have on any given subject, is crucial to understanding what you are thinking and feeling and why you are thinking and feeling what you are. Through my **broader perspective**, I could see the fundamental truth that any given perspective that we may have, *forms the foundation of our* State of Being.

State Of Being

The break-through happened when I realized, that thought, emotion and body state were all bundled into one thing, this became known to me as a **State of Being**. When I would start to meditate, my mind would be moving all over the place like wild fire. But, during these times, I also began to see that not only was my mind busy, but that there was emotion attached to the different thoughts and also a state in my body that came with them. For example, if when I was trying to meditate and I was having thoughts about and argument I had with someone the day before, not only would the thoughts be there, but also the emotions of anger and a physical tension in my body. This became known to me as one complete thing or experience of thought-emotion-body state. I call this a **State of Being**.

As I would be 'trying' to relax and go into a meditation, these different states of being would come and go. It was like they wanted to sit in my driver's seat, so to speak, and drive me; that is, become me or my being-ness. And I discovered that any thought that I would have, would be just another state of being, trying to be me...getting me to identify myself with it. This was when I discovered that I was *not* my thoughts. Thoughts were part of a state of being and if I could relax, I could see that they would come and go. Like little birds flying in and out of view. These states of being were very believable and crafty at trying to convince me that they were me, but I could now see that I was much more.

I began to discover that any and all states of being that I may have, come from some particular perspective.

It's very important to establish, that **State of Being** is known as an experience... as an experiential state. This is an awareness that is made possible through the *broader perspective* that comes from Mindfulness. In other words, I, from this *broader perspective* am 'seeing' the thoughts, feelings and body-state that I am actually having from something like an un-entangled, "3rd person" point of view. It is an awareness that has no time or space; it was outside of time and space. It was through this state of Mindfulness, *and* this 'big inner-eye" (*broader perspective) that* I began to realize something new about the self. I began to discover that any and all states of being that I may have, come from some particular perspective, this insight gave me a freedom that I had never been conscious of before. *I realized that my perspective and thus my state of being could be changed like a pair of shoes!*

*The fact that **Perspective** is the foundation of any **State of Being** means 3 important things for us:*

Perspective is not who we are

1). Perspective as a whole, is a combination 'thing'; and as such, *is not who we are*. Remember what we said in the previous chapter, that Perspective was composed of 3 parts...Perception, Mental View/Attitude and Impression. This is the *understanding* of what Perspective is. <u>We, however, *experience* Perspective as a *State of Being*</u>... as an experience of thought-emotion and body state.

You are not the way you see things. A given Perspective can be so convincing with its thought-emotion-body nature, that in any given moment, it can seem to become who we are. We are always thinking, speaking and doing out of a given mental view/attitude; and we also have the emotions and feelings in our body that go along with this given Perspective. All of this becomes, in our experience, our State of Being. A good example of this can be seen at any sporting event, say a football or basketball game. There are two different teams competing for a win. Each team has its own group of fans. The fans of one team of course want their team to win, so they are screaming and shouting "victory" for their team. These fans are also jumping up and down, and thrusting their arms into the air as they cheer. Not only are they emotional for their team, but their bodies are moving and into the excitement of the moment. All of this will vary during the course of the game, depending on if their team is winning or losing. This is their **State of Being** at the game during that moment.

We, looking at this behavior from a distance, understand they are acting that way because of their **Perspective**. The fans however, are not thinking "this is my perspective"; no, they are in the moment having the *experience* of their Perspective. Namely that they want and believe that their team should win...and they want this quite emphatically! We know that if they were on the other side of the bleachers, their perspective would be different in that they would want the other team to win. This State of Being is not who they are, but in that moment, it is their reality. It is all-consuming; with varying degrees of emotional intensity.

The key here is understanding, like little birds gliding in and out of view, that perspectives/states of being come and go; and are *not* who we are. We are not our thoughts, emotions or body. These are all very important things, but we are not them.

Perspective is localized

2). Meaning that any given perspective or state of being, is what it is based on the person who has it. A person's cultural background, personality, emotional make-up and physical make-up, has everything to do with their perspective. Remember, I'm not talking about the *broader perspective* that comes with mindfulness. I'm referring to any *given* perspective a person may have at the moment, and we know this is expressed in our experience as a **State of Being**.

Someone born in Alaska in 1900 will have a different perspective on computers than someone born in Japan in 1985. Someone who grew up with financial prosperity will have a different outlook on money than someone who grew up poor. Sometimes we don't realize that our perspective is native to who we are, where we grew up, who we are around, etc. We can have a point of view on something, and not really see that we are the only one with that point of view...not everyone else in the world!

Growing up, not many of the people around me were motivated to do something positive in the world, to help bring more awareness and Love into it; I, however, was. My perspective at that time was that, like myself, all of the people around me (or most) wanted to give more Love and awareness to the world, but that was not the case. I saw that different people had different attitudes toward life based, in large part, on who they were.

This sounds to me like I was naïve about people...and I was. However, when it comes to realizing that any given perspective we hold is localized, that it's just our perspective or our larger group's perspective, escapes a lot of people.

Many of us have an attitude or point of view that we fail to realize is just an attitude or point of view. The propaganda in the news media is a good example. We watch the news and we are told of all of the bad and evil things "those people" are doing over there. We get emotional, fired up, start pointing fingers and are ready to go fight and make them pay for being so bad. We feel and believe in every fiber of our being that their destructive, wicked behavior needs to be stopped...corrected. However, this would just be _our_ perspective on them. It would not be _their_ perspective on themselves. We don't know them personally, or what they are doing. Neither have we ever spent any real time with them, to get to know them and their aims.

We point fingers at others, without thinking to point them back at ourselves.

We only 'know' what we 'know' through the news media or other outside sources. We got our thoughts, emotions and the tension in our bodies...our *in the moment* state of being, from outside of ourselves. We get our state of being from an outer source which many times, does not tell the whole story, is biased and is motivating us towards a particular biasness. Instead of us realizing this is just a perspective, we unconsciously or consciously take it as the gospel truth, and build more perspectives around it. This greatly inhibits growth, togetherness and change for the better. We point fingers at others, without thinking to point them back at ourselves. History is littered with this type of behavior. From genocide, to slavery, to religious and scientific persecution, even to profiling the cat down the road, this inability to see that perspective is localized, has caused us to not consciously choose our highest aspirations.

Perspective is Changeable

3). We can have a new attitude about a person, place, and a situation or about life in general. This may at first seem obvious. But how many people do you know that have a certain attitude about something, and it never has changed...even over the years. And that attitude they have, does not serve them...and they will admit that it doesn't. If they truly realized, if they were aware that they could change their perspective, much like changing a pair of shoes, they would do what serves them and simply change their attitude in an instant! This *is* possible, and naturally within your ability to do...it's only the belief...the perspective that it's 'not that easy', that's the reason it may seem like it can't be done that easy.

This fact that Perspective is changeable is our point of departure from a life of knee-jerk responses, disempowerment and randomness, to choosing our lives and living on purpose. Being aware of what state of being we are in will show us what is happening in our lives. Having a perspective and being in a state of being, is by definition, a reality that will be for us as long as we are being. The variable here is that *we get to choose* our

23

perspective and experience different states of being. This is having a mind for life!

Once we have a given perspective, and are in the corresponding state of being, everything that we think, say and do comes out of that place, and our lives become the stuff of that perspective. For example, if I have the point of view that I will be successful in any given activity, I will do things and make moves that I would not do, if I believed the activity was a waste of time. This is why *Mindfulness* and *broader perspective* can be so important in choosing your life consciously; because we will always have some sort of state of being, and we will be acting out of this state of being whether we realize and are aware of it or not. Action is however, only one way in which we live out of our perspectives, which now brings us to our next chapter and a discussion of the *3 Tools*.

Principles

1). **Mindfulness** is a 'place' within you; it is a place of nothingness and at the same time of the infinite.

2). Meditation is <u>any</u> process or activity that brings you into a quiet mind, where an inner peace and clarity dwell.

3). You are *not* your mind.

4). **Broader Perspective** is <u>all </u>choice, <u>all </u>possibility...not just your localized point of view. It is the big inner eye.

5). *Broader Perspective* reveals any given, particular perspective.

6). **State of Being** is defined as being thought, emotion and body state all bundled into one thing.

7). *State of Being* is experiential. It is Perspective experienced.

8). All *States of Being* come from *Perspective*.

9). *States of Being* do and will attempt to drive you.

10). *Perspective* is not who we are.

11). *Perspective* is localized.

12). *Perspective* is changeable.

Nathan Wallace

Chapter 3

The 3 Tools

Thought, Word and Action

The 3 Tools of creation are **Thought, Word and Action.** Much has been said on these in many books, ancient and modern; and I could write volumes of books on each one of these tools. But for our purposes, I'll keep it as a very brief overview; just high-lighting these ideas within the context of our discussion. My point here, with these tools, is that they are the <u>means</u> by which your Perspective manifests in the outer world and creates real-ity. These tools are also the means by which the outer world aligns with us and our Perspective to create a reality; a reality that matches or is in tune with our *Perspective* and *State of Being*.

Thought

Thought is more than just thinking. I define thought as any mo-vement of inner mind conscious awareness. This could be rea-soning, imagination, planning, fantasizing, considering, intuiting, visualizing and so on. And by our definition, thought also includes all of the functions of the body that seem to be 'automatic'. Such automatic functions as the operation of the autonomic nervous system, healing of wounds and disease, growing of finger nails, hair and so on. These bodily processes have been called 'unconscious' in years past by science, but they were wrong. Each of these processes have awareness, has mind consciousness of their own. This is why they know what to do and when to do it without you consciously telling them. You don't have to tell your heart to beat or your hair to grow, nor do you know how your scar heals, but your body does, and it does it. So we see that thought does not just happen in the physical brain.

All thought springs from a perspective

Thought is born from and possess the nature of the perspective from which it derives. Thought also translates your perspective into everyday life. Thought also goes to work to carry out and translate your perspective into your life experience. And because the thought is a product of the perspective, the stuff in the outer world that gets drawn, matches not only the vibration of the thought, but the outer 'stuff' matches up with the perspective as well. *This is where a lot of the creating and choosing in life comes from, and where it all starts.*

It's like having things drawn into your life on automatic, and you may not be able to figure out why you're getting what you're getting. It's because your thoughts, just within their own nature, within their own right, have a vibrational nature that matches up with other compatible vibrational natures of other thoughts, attitudes, people, places, things, situations, etc. This is a creating that you do not deliberately do. Your power is not in governing the laws of vibration... that has its own rules. Your power is in choosing your perspective...that is your job.

So by <u>deliberately</u> holding a perspective means also that your thoughts now will fall in line with your mental view and attitudes; which in turn means that other thoughts, feelings, as well as people, things and situations in the outer world, will again fall in line with your mental view and attitudes...your perspective. It's like a big circle. You are now creating by what I call, *deliberate default*. You are creating just by the perspective you have chosen, and thus your thoughts. This is an effortless choosing, where life lines up with you just because of how you think, or your *general* state of mind.

Thought moving outward to create in the 3-D world, is something I think we in general are very familiar with in terms of its function, the way it works. In other words, I have a thought about something...say hanging up the phone, then I press the button and hang it up...it's just that simple. I think of what I want to say, and then I say it. Thought is still at work translating my perspective, this time outward into the 3-D world.

I wake up with *thoughts* of gratitude for the day God has given me. I feel strong, and inspired for the day ahead. My thoughts and feelings are accruing other thoughts and feelings along these lines, and I'm feeling stronger, with more inner joy. Seemingly out of nowhere, I get some really great ideas for a new project I'm working on...the momentum is growing; and then as I walk out the door to go outside... Ouch! I stub my toe! I look at it, it hurts but its ok, it doesn't throw my mood off. I'm grateful that it's not really hurt, and I keep stepping on my way. *This is invincibility.*

Word

Word is the spoken communication that comes out of your mouth ...talking. The power of the words that you use has been recognized for centuries as a creative force. I'm sure most of us have heard that 'life and death are in the power of the tongue', this is ancient wisdom. We know the feelings and effects that words can have when we use them or hear them in our personal relationships, jobs, etc. Words, as a creation of man and as interrelated with man, carry their own energy nature; this has been found to be quantifiable. There have even been scientific experiments showing the effect of words on water.

Yet in my day to day life, I see how careless many of us can be with our words. We say things we don't mean that can hurt someone else, and even damage a relationship. But what is even bigger than that, is how we use words when we describe ourselves..."I'm no good", "I can't do that", "I'll never make it", etc.; little do we know that words have the power to create. Just as thought carries a vibrational frequency, words do as well. By their very nature, words attract unto themselves other words, things, people, mindsets and situations that are like unto themselves.

Words create not only based on the word being used, but also based upon the energy behind the word.

Our thoughts manifest themselves through our words, and remember our thoughts have their basis in our perspective. Words create not only based on the word being used, but also based upon the energy *behind* the word. The energy behind the word is based upon...you guessed it...your perspective, your attitude. For example, if I say to someone, "please put this over there", those words are instructions designed to have an action accomplished in the outer world. Now in addition to the raw information that the words themselves carry, there is also energy behind those words. Based on my *attitude*, if it is good and happy, the words are going to come across much different than if my attitude is bad because of whatever; and the person that I'm speaking to will pick this up immediately. When the person hears my words and if the energy behind them is bad, the person may confront me, they may not do what I asked or if they do it, they may now do it with bad energy themselves and make me more angry! And the situation could escalate from there. The opposite could manifest as well, by me asking with good energy. I'm sure you can pick up on someone's 'vibe' when they talk to you; and that vibe that you feel is coming from their attitude/mental view, in other words their perspective.

Action

Action is about a physical doing. Many people think of this as the main way to create... going out there and 'doing' in order to make things happen. While the other tools of thought and word are just as powerful, action does put the icing on the cake. For example, my idea to write and compose a song will not cause you to be able to hear it...I must take action to manifest it *into* this material world. In my mind I actually have already created the song... I can hear all of its music and vocals with my 'inner ear'. But until I pick up a microphone, instruments, etc., and do the action-work, it will just remain an idea.

Action, just like thought and word, has an energy or vibe to it as well.

One person sings a song and it's okay, but kind of bland. Then another person comes up and sings the same song with passion, sweeping us up into the emotion of the song. Both are doing the same action, but they both have two different energies behind what they do. As a result the actions of the two singers have different effects and impressions on the people listening and on the atmosphere. The effects could range from the people getting tired and going home, to them becoming more festive...buying more food and drinks and socializing more. Action translates Perspective into the outer world and elicits a response back from the outer world just as thought and word.

In the last two chapters, I wanted to establish with you that *Mindfulness*, as leading to a place of inner awareness, is really a major key to choosing your life; and that we do the actual choosing of our lives using the 3 Tools of thought, word and action. We also choose by the nature or vibration of these 3 tools as they spring from our perspective... whether we are aware of it or not. If we have a mind for life, we are aware through our *broader perspective*, of what particular perspective we are holding; and if that perspective serves our higher selves, then thinking, speaking and doing out of that is a good thing. However, if we are not aware of our inner perspectives, our thoughts, words and deeds are not serving our highest aspirations and at best are producing a random life.

I also want to point out something very interesting and insightful about these 3 tools. We have now seen that these 3 tools (thought, word and action) have a dual function. On the one hand, the tools translate our *state of being*, and therefore our perspective outward into the outer 3-D world. We also have seen that because of their energy-nature, their vibe, they draw back to us people, ideas, and situations that match up with them. But there is also a third way these tools can work as well. *These 3 tools can be extended and turned inward and used to change our perspectives!* I will present this in terms of various practical techniques in a later chapter.

What I'm going to be doing now is taking a turn towards what I call: 'every day personal transformation'. I want to help you to get to a place of deliberate choosing *in the midst* of your everyday life. While Mindfulness is a more thorough way to create change within yourself because you become <u>directly</u> aware of what perspectives you hold; not everyone has the opportunity or the *time* to go within and meditate. In fact many people are reading this book because they are in the middle of different situations that they want to improve, and they can't stop their lives to go get Mindful!

So in the following chapters, I will begin to highlight some ways you can get your life going in a more deliberate and fulfilling direction, <u>using techniques that don't require you to necessarily meditate;</u> to meditate, that is, even by our broad definition of it. But before we get into these techniques, I want to bring out for you, the differences between choosing your life *directly* and *indirectly*. I believe that having a bit more clarity on this will create a perfect launching pad for these practical, everyday techniques.

Who doesn't want a fulfilling, prosperous life? Your relationships can be rewarding for everyone involved. Your finances can be more than enough. Your health and body can be in tip top shape. All of these virtues are your birthright and you really *do* have the power already within you, to have the best that life has to offer!

<u>Principles</u>

1). *The 3 Tools* of creation are *Thought, Word and Action*.

2). The 3 Tools are the means by which Perspective manifests itself into the outer world.

3). The 3 Tools also draw, due to their energy-nature, aspects of the outer and inner world back to themselves. This is ultimately drawing back to our perspective, and therefore our lives and who we are.

4). *Thought* is more than just thinking; it is as any movement of inner mind conscious awareness.

5). Thought, as well as all the tools, derives from Perspective.

6). **Word** is the spoken communication that comes out of your mouth ...talking.

7). Words create based on the meaning of the definition of the word, and also the energy behind the word, it's 'vibe'.

8). **Action** is about a physical doing.

9). Actions are typically seen as the main way to get things done; and while Action is a great and irreplaceable tool, all 3 tools are equivalent in their creative power.

Chapter 4

The Mind to Choose

You are living your life through various perspectives. Everything that you are thinking, saying and doing, by your will in the outer world, comes from a mental view or attitude that you have. Everything that is happening *to* you is happening *to* you because of the mental view or attitude you have. We established this in the last two chapters. Life and its situations may appear to be happening without your consent, or even randomly, and to your unaware mind, they are. And thus you were responding to life in a 'knee-jerk' way. But that ceases to be the case once you are aware of what perspective(s) you are holding; and even *more* importantly...that you can *deliberately choose* your perspective!

As I have said before, one of your greatest gifts, as a creation of God, is your ability to behold. To not only have *Perspective*, but to be able to *impress* it and to be able to change it...at will. We *impress* our mental views all day long; the thing is we don't always realize what perspective we are holding within ourselves on any given subject. So our thoughts, words and actions are coming from an inner view that we are not really clear about. So we think, say and do things that we really don't mean, or that put us in situations that we don't want to be in.

Taking massive action is how people are accustomed to changing their lives for the better; on the surface this seems right, especially given how powerful a tool action is. However, this is the wrong approach; massive action within itself will not essentially change a thing. Appearances will change, but the substance will remain the same...year after year.

Deliberate clarity of Perspective, is what brings the 3 tools of thought, word and action together.

For true, wholesome change to take place in your life, your thoughts, words and actions must line up together and be on one accord. A house divided against itself cannot stand. This is so even at a most basic level. For example, when a friend and I are walking down the street, and we arrive at the corner, if we should turn right, I have the thought to turn right, I then say to my friend "this is where we turn", I look that way and I make my body turn in that direction. My thought, word and action line up, so I end up turning right. Have you ever arrived at a corner or a fork in the road and wasn't sure which way to go? Maybe your body started going one way, but your thought was pulling you in an opposite direction...it feels really weird and can throw you off balance even!

This happens at all levels. I know someone who has been in several bad romances...in a row. She says she doesn't like them and that she wants to be in a good relationship. As time passes, and we speak again, she tells me about her new "romance" and guess what...it's bad! She's crying on my shoulder about how bad it is, and that she wants to get out. But then the next day she's right back in that bad relationship again! What she's saying to me about wanting to get out of her current bad relationship (and have a good relationship with someone else) does not match up with her actions. In this case, there is an inner perspective that doesn't allow for her thoughts, words and actions to work together. Maybe she has the attitude that she can't get anyone else or maybe her mental view about her-self is that she is unattractive physically, etc.; etc.

You choose your life by choosing your perspective and letting your thoughts, words and deeds come from that place.

It's really that simple. To some, this may sound passive, but it's not. By being conscious and deliberately choosing what perspective you hold on any given subject, you're automatically setting up the vibe and direction of your thoughts, words and actions; which will also govern what gets drawn to you. *You* are also shaping how they will manifest in your outer experience. If a person works harder changing the action only, nothing really changes; the same could be said of thought and word. It's only when a deliberate *choosing* of Perspective occurs, that there is a real change in outer manifestation of thought, word and action. A new *state of being* will also be experienced as well.

So how is it that you deliberately choose your perspective?
You deliberately choose your perspective
either <u>Directly</u> or <u>Indirectly</u>:

1). <u>Directly</u>: The first step in choosing your perspective directly, is by becoming totally conscious, totally aware of what it is; then you decide to take on a new one...a new attitude, a new point of view. This can occur in a meditative-type state like I described to you in chapter 2; or through any way that gives you an inner *revelation* on the way you truly see, and the way you truly feel about something. Once you see this truth about yourself, in its naked honesty, you will have clarity and can decide to stay with that point of view or choose a different point of view based on what you want. This type of choosing happens through an inner awareness of what the given perspective is, and then you decide on a different perspective. So, just becoming conscious of whatever perspective you hold....is *not* doing the choosing. Awareness itself is **not** equal to choosing.

...a temperature does not cause a cold or flu.

So for example, I'm playing an instrument and my mind begins to simplify and quiet down, as was described in an earlier chapter. During this time, I get an insight about myself; for example, I see that I over-dress in the spring time because I'm afraid of getting sick. Well, I don't want to over dress in the spring, and I already know, from being a trained scientist, that a temperature does not cause a cold or flu. So now the gig is over and I stop playing my instrument, but I now know of a perspective that I was not aware of before. Before I thought I over-dressed in the spring time because I wanted to make sure I was warm. But now, I have an awareness on why I *really* over-dress in the spring...It's because I have a perspective, a mental view that chilly spring air will make me catch a cold or flu. This I know logically and through experience as well, to *not* be true.

So what do I do with this newly found awareness? In order to actively choose in the sense in which we are talking about, I decide to **not** subscribe to that old point of view any more. My new perspective is based more so on what I know to be true, rather than on ideas that were imprinted on me; and ideas that I randomly picked up (unknowingly) from friends, family, the media and so on. My new perspective is that temperature, in itself, does not cause me to get a cold or flu. This new perspective serves me much better, and I also know it to be true. So as a result, my actions, and even my thoughts and words change on this subject. I start dressing lighter for the spring than I did in the winter. I begin to appreciate and talk about how beautiful the spring time is. I'm also more cheerful to other people on the street... I have a 'glow' about me. I then make new friends and so on.

Here, I got the _**direct awareness**_ of my perspective and I _deliberately_ choose a different one. This then led to a different _state of being_; which in turn led to different thoughts, words and actions translating this new perspective outward, into the outer 3-D world. Different thoughts, words and actions, by default (because of their energy), caused my outer experience to be more of what I wanted...people saw my 'glow' and were **attracted**. So I then made new personal and professional relations as a result. This domino-effect of goodness just goes on and on, inward and outward...outward and inward.

2). Indirectly: In order to choose our perspective _indirectly_, we don't _always_ have to be aware of what the perspective is within itself. All we need to know is that we want things to be different in our lives. In order to change a given perspective deliberately but indirectly, we use _Techniques_. Many of which, I will show you very shortly.

Think of it like flipping the light switch on when you go into your bedroom. You walk into your room, flip the switch and you've got light. You are not aware of all of the many wires and electrical connections inside and outside of your home that allow the light to come on. Nor are you aware of where all of those wires and their electrical current go once they leave your neighborhood block. In fact, we may not even be clear on exactly what electricity actually is. But guess what, we don't need to! We don't need to have an awareness of any of these things to change the room from dark to light! All we do is use the technique of flipping the switch, and there the light is!

This lighter approach is why I find this to be the most effective way for most people. People are already in the midst of whatever relationships and situations they are in. People are also busy doing a lot of stuff; so much so, that it can be difficult and an inconvenience to go off somewhere and go into the silence. That's why I tend to emphasize this *indirect* method more so. If the majority of people are leading busy lives, they don't have time for the *direct* method of deliberately choosing their perspectives, let alone to dive deep and understand the inner processes at work, as described in earlier chapters. Of course the *direct* method is just as valuable, but it's not for everyone. Both are presented in this book so that you can choose how you want to use them.

With the Indirect method, you don't have to be aware of what inner mental view and attitude you really have...

Using *techniques* to deliberately choose your perspective is indirect, because as we said earlier, you don't have to be aware of what inner mental view and attitude you really have towards some person, place, situation or thing. Indeed, as I have been saying rather emphatically in this book...many times we don't really know what the true, inner perspective we hold on something is anyway! What we do see, however, is that our lives are not what we want, or all that they could be. Or at least there are a few things going on in our lives that could change for the better.

Remember that all of the things going on in your life are ultimately due to a given perspective that you have.

So in this *indirect* method, we don't have to dive deep and become aware of what the perspective is. No, all we have to do is know we want things to be better, and how we want them to be better…then use the techniques to, in-effect, deliberately choose a new perspective. All we have to do is flip the switch to turn the light on!

So let's take the technique of *Gratitude*, which I will present in the next chapter. I know, for example, that there is someone on my job that irritates me. I get irritated because I feel they are obnoxious and pushy. They care more about who they are, what they can do and what they want…more so than what the company wants from us all. Of course, this tries my patience, and of course…irritates the heck out of me. Not only do I have to do my job, but I have to deal with this person as well! So it bothers me and I get irritated and I complain. I complain to myself, I complain to the other co-workers, I complain to my friends and family away from the job. All of this complaining just makes everything worse.

I'm so busy with my day to day life, that I just don't have time to get into the *direct* way of choosing my perspective. But I *can* still use the technique of Gratitude to change my perspective on the situation, thus changing my inner self (my *state of being*) as well …this is using the *indirect* way. So when I wake up in the morning, as I'm getting dressed for work, I express gratitude for this person. At first it seems and feels weird, considering how much this person irritates me. But after a little while, I get an insight…an "*ah-ha moment*"! I begin to see this person somewhat differently. I start to recognize this person's irritating behavior as a means for me to develop. I now see their behavior as a means for me to develop patience, composure, poise, focus and even the ability for me to confront someone in a peaceful an effective way. What a gift this person is in my life!

What has happened here is that by using the technique of gratitude I have indirectly, but deliberately, chosen a new perspective on this person's behavior. Before, the perspective I had of them (that they were irritating) was not serving me. Now however, my perspective has shifted to them being a gift. It's the same person doing the same stuff, but now I welcome each interaction with them as an opportunity for growth! We may even become friends in the process!

You see with this indirect way of choosing my perspective, I didn't have to quiet my mind down and allow my *broader perspective* to show me things at all. In fact, I chose a new point of view and attitude on the situation while I was getting dressed in the morning! I knew I wanted a better experience with this person at work, and all I did was use a technique... that's it!

Positive Expectancy

We are creatures of emotion feeling. In order for any technique to create real change within us, we need to put feeling into what we do. We need to allow feelings to radiate through us, the techniques that we use and in our lives. This is what it means to have *soul*...to be soulful. Cold logical application of concepts or techniques is very dry, bland, and colorless; and will not inspire our hearts and minds to transform. This is the reason why so many people start on programs of self-improvement and quit. They are doing all of this stuff that they are told to do to make things better, but they aren't feeling any of it...and that's the honest truth!

We are colorful creatures with vibrant emotional expression, as well as logic! Every concept and technique must be understood **and** felt. Your transformation *is* personal; you must make it so and take this whole thing personally. There are two ways to feel that will aid in the bringing about of what you want:

1). Emotions. Feel within your emotions. Our emotions have a broad range, happy, excited, eager, surprised, etc.

2). Physical body. The physical sensations need to be a part of your experience when you are doing the techniques. So for example, if you are visualizing surfing on the beach, as part of what you want to do, then you need to 'feel', through the visualizing. Feel the water splashing on your feet, the heat of the sun on your skin, the taste of salt water on your lips, and so on.

Feeling through your emotions and physical body, will give flesh and blood to your use of the techniques. Feeling will also *move* you and your 3 tools of thought, word and action into making what you want for yourself a reality.

Out of all of the feelings you could feel, **Positive Expectancy**, is of key importance. Positive Expectancy is a fresh, anticipation-feeling for what you desire to happen as having **already** happened and being yours already. You already own it, and you are feeling how good it feels to have it, be there, etc. It is not the same as hoping or 'positive thinking'. With Positive Expectancy, you are not hoping for anything to happen. Nor are you straining your brains to think positive. There is nothing to hope for, and there is nothing that you need to think positive about to try and make happen.

You are excited that you 'have it' already and are feeling the emotion and physical sensations of already having it.

With Positive Expectancy, you already know that whatever you want is already done, and in the process of coming into your experience. You are excited that you 'have it' already and are feeling the emotion and physical sensations of already having it. It's like being excited to know that an item you ordered has already been shipped and is on the way. You already know it's been shipped, and you just can't wait to get it. So in the surfer example I gave above, you are happy and excited about being on the beach, you feel the ocean water caress your body, etc.

So now you should have a good understanding and feel for the fundamental principles and concepts, as well as how we go about doing the choosing. Just this information alone is dynamite! This is enough to spark a revolution in your life! But let's take this whole thing a step further and get into some practical techniques that you can use in your everyday life…on the wing. These techniques will help you, even more so, to live a life of abundance; *and* a life of unapologetic authenticity!

Principles

1). You live your life through various perspectives.

2). Everything that is happening *to* you in your life experience is happening *to* you because of the mental view or attitude you have.

3). Deliberate clarity of Perspective is what brings the 3 tools of thought, word and action together.

4). You choose your perspective either **Directly** or **Indirectly.**

5). In this book we focus more on the *Indirect Method* of choosing Perspective, because it can fit in with many people's busy life style, being done in the midst of their daily activities.

6). Feelings and allowing feelings to manifest, is of <u>paramount importance</u> in using the techniques, and ultimately choosing and living the life we want; this is a big part of having a mind for life.

7). Within our approach, there are two ways to feel: with the **Emotions** and with the **Physical Body**.

8). **Positive Expectancy** is a fresh, anticipation-feeling for what you desire to happen as having <u>already</u> happened and being yours already. This is a 'felt' experience in the emotions and physical body.

Chapter 5

Techniques for Living

Every significant break-through is the result of a change in Perspective.

The "ah-ha" moment, the "lightbulb" going off, is the result of a change in Perspective. This happens on all levels of human existence. From Einstein riding the beam of light in a dream, which lead to his break-through in Physics; to the chef who comes up with a new way to make avocado stir-fry; mere action, even words or thoughts, are not enough *in their own right* to create real change. Notice I say 'in their own right' because there are ways in which we can purposefully use the 3 tools of thought, word and action to provoke a change in perspective. We will be going over this shortly...when we get to the discussion on techniques. This kind of break-through is often referred to as *'Paradigm Shift'*. A *paradigm shift* tends to be looked upon as happening randomly, but actually these shifts can happen at any time...on purpose! No longer do we have to wait on some lightning rod of genius from the clouds to advance our personal lives, relationships, finances or even our existence as a species. The ability to choose *is* within your grasp!

Face Reality

Before we get into these techniques, I need to say something to you about reality. Reality is real. There is nothing more important than for you to face reality. *This book will be totally ineffective for you unless you can face reality.* You are where you are. The world you see around you... your relationships, your physical possessions, your health, your neighborhood, your bills...all of these things are reality, and constitute your picture and experience of it. If you have a problem facing reality, this book is *not* for you. If for example, you want to lose weight by only picturing yourself skinny, you are going to stay fat. If you want to become financially independent, so you quit your job and repeat to yourself "I'm rich, I'm rich, I'm rich", all day long...you will soon be homeless. This is being foolish.

You must not only face reality, but you must confront it.

This book and its techniques are designed to help you confront reality. This book is in your hands to not only aid you in confronting reality, but transforming it. YOU are the change agent! *YOU have the power already within you to create and even destroy worlds...*this is your birthright! Once you are committed to changing your life, there is nothing or no one that can stop you!

Facing reality is the first step towards getting to where you want to be in life. So by all means, face reality. Face it and take it in, but also know that it is in your power to change it. This *feeling* of being empowered within you *is* the 'juice' that makes all of these techniques spring to life. Never accept less, because you do not have to! **It is irresponsible for you to accept a version of reality that does not serve you.** Often times other people, or even the media, want to *impress* a reality upon you that either is the way *they* see the world, or the way *they* want you to see the world. But I'm here to tell you, that YOU have full choice on how YOU see the world. How you see the world will determine what you think, say and do. *The only Reality that is spelled with* *a capital R, meaning that it is absolute and unchangeable, is God.* Anything else that is said to be "reality" is under your authority...it is fair game! That being said, on to making some changes...

Techniques

Here I will give to you techniques on how to deliberately choose your perspective on any given subject. These techniques are based on the *indirect* way of choosing your perspective. The *indirect* way of choosing your perspective was explained in detail in the previous chapter; please refer back to it if you need a refresher.

Put your heart into these Techniques...understand them and feel them in your emotions and physical body.

It's very important for me to say here at the outset that these techniques are to be done with <u>all</u> of you. You must not only use some understanding, but you must *feel* what you are doing, saying and thinking. Even if the technique is something that you can do while taking a 5 minute shower, get into the habit of feeling what you are doing **within your emotions and your physical body.** This will cause whatever you want to happen, to take place with vividness, power and effectiveness! Logic, however powerful, is one- dimensional and used by itself will *not* create real change. Remember the example of the two singers that I gave earlier? One singer sang without passion, and the other did? Well the same thing applies here...feel what you do. Surrender and put your soul into it.

It's my belief that most people, deep down, want the best for themselves. Just getting the understandings and insights from the book up to this point, is really all it takes for you to start the choosing. You have been using the 3 Tools all along anyway, and been having perspectives on different things all of your life. Just the revelation of the nature and mechanics of Perspective, as were presented previously in this book, is enough for most people to hit the ground running. The following techniques are really an enhancement to the main text. So make sure you have read the entire book before you get into these techniques.

In order to choose and have a mind for *your* life, you must have perspectives that serve you. To choose the perspectives that allow you to grow and prosper in life, you must know what growth and prosperity means for *you* in particular. You must know where you want to go, what you want to be in life, what you want to achieve. This understanding of what you want to be, do and have, will allow you to know what perspectives will serve you best. This understanding is a very personal thing, which only you can work out. That being said...

1). Express Gratitude:

Become grateful. Become grateful with not only your words, but with your emotions and the feeling in your body as well. Genuine gratitude is a tremendous vehicle of change! Gratitude is *not* just a 'warm and fuzzy' feeling! Begin to practice being grateful...for what you have and for what you don't have. Practice being grateful for what you want... and what you don't want; for the 'good' and the 'bad'. The first thing to do when you wake up is to express your gratitude. Express your appreciation for the smallest things...just waking up is something to be grateful for. Also move yourself to express *genuine* gratitude for the people, situations, things, etc., that you believe you do not want. This will cause the following:

A). You will become aware of what perspective you hold on whatever you express gratitude towards.

You may have never before realized how much you dislike something or someone in your life until you try and express gratitude towards them. This also works in reverse, by expressing gratitude, you will see how truly significant this person or situation is to you. ***Gratitude, by its nature, brings the light of consciousness into all aspects of the self.***

Gratitude is a form of confrontation!

B). Your perspective will change towards whatever you considered unwanted in your life.

The stuff in your life that bothered you and you hated, didn't want or didn't like, will lose its sting...it will lose its power over you. You will see these 'bad' things from a different angle. This new perspective will reveal the unwanted to you as gifts, as helpers in your growth and development. This is invincibility! This then is *not* the same thing as you accepting what you don't want in your life, not at all. In fact, no one teaches this, but as quiet as it's kept...Gratitude is a form of confrontation! This is a powerful revelation! This is a technique that will overcome any obstacle! Placing gratitude towards the unwanted in your life is you confronting and transforming it. It is you affirming that you are larger than your problems, and that in the end you are victorious...in spite of them! You are acting courageously, and that courage is grounded in Love.

Doing this first thing in the morning, is about you facing your daily life with the power of Love...which Gratitude ultimately is!

2). Visualize:

Visualizing is using inner sight in a deliberate way to envision a thing, scenario, place, person, etc. Close your eyes and picture your cell phone. You see this everyday so it should be easy to see. In your mind's eye, look at the front of it; now turn it over and look at the back. I want you to now, still visualizing it, turn it on. What does the home screen look like? Doing this, you have just engaged in visualizing. We can use this to choose a new perspective based on what we want out of life in the following ways...

A). Pre-Pave what you want for the day:

After you wake up and have given some Gratitude, *Pre-Pave* what you want your day to be like. This technique can be done while you're taking a shower, getting dressed, etc. You do this pre-paving by visualizing how you want things to unfold during the course of the day; and feeling in your emotions and physical body how the things feel that you want to have happen. You must make it a complete little experience for yourself. For example, visualize yourself getting to work on time, and feeling happy to see your co-workers. This is a good start. Now continue to visualize and include, having a good lunch and having a productive, energized output at work, in all of its details. Continue visualizing how you want your entire day to unfold. Keep visualizing until you see yourself back home getting ready for bed.

What you are doing here is using visualization to pre-pave, in advance, how you want your day to be. You are doing this according to what you want for yourself and others. Your desires, attitudes and aspirations are always about the perspective you have. By pre-paving your day like this, you are choosing your perspective and deliberately *impressing* it on your day. This technique is powerful in that you are setting up a wonderful day, even before you walk out the door!

B). Visualize the big picture:

See in your mind's eye *what you want to be, do and have* with as much feeling, definition and clarity as possible. Just generating an inner view such as this will ultimately shift you into a perspective that serves you. You will also notice that your *state of being* will change to be in accordance with the perspective; and remember the perspective was generated because you used this technique of visualizing. In doing this type of visualizing, you are envisioning a larger goal that you want to achieve; as opposed to something small. As an example, it's the middle of the winter and you're in the Midwestern United States, say Illinois. Now visualize traveling to a favorite sunny spot, it could be the Caribbean, California, etc. You must visualize every detail, from going online and booking the trip, to packing your bags, to traveling to the airport. Visualize yourself all the way there. When you get there, what are you doing? Lying on the beach? Meeting up with friends? Going to a concert? Also allow to emerge in this visualization, how you feel in your emotions and physical body. Are you feeling, happy, eager? When the plane is taking off do you feel excited or nervous? Is the sun hitting your face? Is it hot there? Can you taste the mango juice?

It should be like a little movie going on inside of you, very vivid and colorful, with emotions and feelings in your body as well.

Make the imagery very real and detailed, in your mind's eye. Allow yourself to experience all the feelings of emotion and body state that comes into the inner images. It should be like a little movie going on inside of you, very vivid and colorful, with emotions and feelings in your body as well. By you doing this, you have shifted your inner perspective; and your *state of being* will show you this by matching up with it. So when you visualize yourself at the airport, you may feel excited that you're leaving. Or you may feel stressed out from so many people being around, etc. These *states of being* have grown out of what you have done with the visualizing.

During this or any visualization, you can learn a lot from the perspective that you generate. You can learn what kind of perspective is best for you based on how you think and *feel (state of being)* during the visualization. For example, you're visualizing that you're in the airport and you feel stressed. This is a good indicator that you should shift your perspective on how you see airports, and even groups of people, so that your state of being will change. Then when you go to the airport, in real-life, you don't have any stress. The technique of Visualization introduces us to a creative world where we get to try on different perspectives, relative to our goals, desires and aspirations. In this place we can become aware of what perspectives work for us, and choose the ones that serve our highest aspirations.

3). Play Pretend... *for-real*:

This technique has a lot to do with visualizing; except for one thing...you are actually living out in the 3-D world, what you visualized! Just like children do, and just like you used to do when you were a kid. The only thing is that pretending as an adult is much more fun! As an adult, you know what's going on; and you're playing pretend in order to have even more fun.

So just like with the Visualizing technique, you start with knowing what you want to be, do and have. With this knowledge, you visualize yourself <u>already</u> being it, doing it and having it. The greater the detail in which you visualize, the better. The greater your feelings of emotion and body are when you visualize, the better. *This technique cannot be effective with just creating pictures in your mind only; emotion and body feelings must be allowed to flow and have full bloom within the visualizing!* Visualize until the *state of being* emerges that matches up with what you are visualizing. You will now have visualized yourself into a new perspective, but don't just stop there. Take this new attitude into your everyday life and affairs, and pretend to be what you want to be...and *pretend for-real*.

You want to be a billionaire? Visualize yourself into how that *feels*; believe it or not, your soul has the ability to do that. How would a billionaire respond to situations? How have you been responding to situations now, not being a billionaire? What's the difference? Would a billionaire get stressed out over spending 5 dollars on a sandwich that they really wanted to eat? Would a billionaire (already being a billionaire) allow themselves to be mistreated and taken advantage of, just to make a few bucks? How does the texture of the physical money feel to your fingertips, now that you are a billionaire? What is your attitude towards money now? Perhaps money feels less important to you now from when you were poor. These questions are always answered from a certain perspective. Whatever you want to live, experience or accomplish in your life, visualize (with feeling) yourself already having and doing those things... but don't stop there, <u>go straight to being in your everyday life!</u> Using this billionaire example, walk and talk according to the *state of being* that emerges from your visualizations of being a billionaire. Your thoughts, words and actions will be matching that billionaire perspective and translate, as well as draw to you based on that perspective. We discussed this process in an earlier chapter. Doing this, you then will be playing pretend...for real.

Some people think that to be able to be something, they need to do stuff and have stuff first, but that's wrong.

The point of view that you have to kill yourself working hard to become what you want is incomplete. That is placing action far above your other tools of thought and word. Working hard, taking massive action is great and very important. However, if your words and thoughts are not on one accord, all of that back-breaking effort will not allow you to become what you want, or maintain and grow the little that you might achieve. Some people think that to be able to be something, they need to do stuff and have stuff first, but that's wrong. For example, if I want to prosper in my business I can have the view that I need a lot of money first so I can buy the different things I need. I don't have the money I need to buy stuff, so I feel like it cannot be done until I have the startup money. But this perspective will not allow me to get started in my business.

This is why so many people start and stop on their goals and dreams, over and over again, year after year. At some point, I will have to take on a different point of view about getting my business started. Because just to say 'I don't have the money in order to have and do what I need to do', will never allow me to become a business owner. At some point I will have to see *how* I can work with what I have already, no matter how small it is, and build from there. What I *do* have to work with could be time, money, contacts, creative ideas, etc. When I start *being* the person who works and begins with what they have, I have stopped *being* the person who says 'I need this or that in order to even start'. A shift in perspective has taken place. This technique of 'Play Pretend' is a great way to achieve a new perspective like this.

See, when you can actually experience the *state of being* that comes with achieving what you want to be, do or have, it will be very exciting and exhilarating! You just won't want to go back to that dark and drab place of wanting and not having... of being needy! All you have to do is stay in that powerful, exciting *state of being* and...

A). Ideas will come to you. Not just any old ideas either; but ideas to put into motion that will allow you to be and accomplish what you want!

B). You will begin to **speak** to others and yourself differently! Your words will carry authority and power. You will be talking about *how* you can accomplish things, instead of how you can't! You will be speaking with a strong sense of hope, health and faith. You will, by default, be inspiring other people; and automatically drawing more good to yourself and the people in your life!

C). You will **do** things that you didn't think of doing before! You will make moves that you didn't have the confidence to make before! And the moves you do make will be on point...no more flailing your fists wildly into the air! You will do much less action, and get humongous results! This is the way of prosperity.

The Play Pretend technique is very powerful and transformative. Many successful people have and do use it all the time. Use it until it becomes second nature for you.

4). Swap and Walk:

This technique is about understanding the perspective of another. With the **Swap and Walk** technique, you *Swap* places with someone else and you *Walk* in their shoes for a change. You see the world from their perspective. You *feel* what they *feel*. How much better a world we would have if we could sometimes get out of our own heads. In order to understand what someone else is going through... what someone else is dealing with!

We want to evolve as a species beyond fear, domination and control.

You see, these techniques I'm giving you, are <u>not</u> really about getting stuff. Ultimately we want a better world. We want to evolve past the abuse of the earth and its creatures; and to evolve as a species beyond fear, domination and control. So when we set our sights on becoming our greatest version, our highest ideal of ourselves, we *are* heading in the right direction. Also I would say, understanding the perspective of another person, group or nation is *also* a step in the right direction.

This is a very powerful technique because it can bring healing to our personal relationships and the world at large. Aside from healing, it can bring us closer to one another.

When I say you *swap* places with someone else, I don't mean literally. I mean you make a sincere effort to see their perspective on any given subject. Remember, their perspective will be expressed through their thoughts, words and actions. So when you talk to them and spend time with them, you will see their perspective.

When I say walk in their shoes, I mean see and <u>feel</u> the world through <u>their</u> eyes.

We know that every perspective has its corresponding *state of being*. So as you see things from their mental view, you will feel what they feel. You will also understand their thoughts and their rationale for doing what they do. This is not to say that you have to agree with them. You are taking on their perspective to understand them, at the very least. Now if it's a personal relationship where you are intimately involved with this person, this technique can work wonders.

The 'how' of using this technique is simple and easy to grasp. The process is essentially the same for any group or individual that you may want to feel and understand. Let's take an intimate relationship, as an example. Your partner seems to be distant and not as affectionate as usual. You think it's because of the large project they are busy on. So time passes, the project has been completed, and they still are acting distant and cold. So you think about it for a while and you come to the conclusion that you need to be at home more. So you rearrange your schedule to be there more, and that doesn't work. You still, are totally in your own head.

Finally, you go and talk to your partner about it and you find out that your partner had a tragedy in their family a couple weeks prior. During your talk, your partner expressed how they felt about the tragedy to you. The tragedy made them feel depressed and withdrawn; they felt a deep inner sadness. You are listening to this, and you can *feel* what they feel. At this point, you also *understand* why they were acting cold and distant. You just had a perspective shift. Now everything feels better in the relationship because, not only can you feel and understand it from their point of view, but you also allow them their space to heal.

This is a marvelous technique for getting out of your own skin and truly understanding someone else.

5). Flip the Hat:

The Flip the Hat technique is a process where you take on the perspective of a position or role that you want to play or learn more about. This is not about understanding a person, but it's about understanding a perspective that goes with a role or position. For example, a role as a manager, doctor, teacher, housewife, etc., that you are curious in learning more about, or that you think you might want to take on. You are flipping your hat from one perspective to another, and all of these different perspectives are connected with different roles or positions. So the hat you wear everyday may be 'mom', this is your normal everyday role. Well you might be interested in creating a business, so you would flip on another hat called 'CEO'. Keep in mind that it's not the title of the position or role that matters; but it's the perspective that goes with that title or position that you are after.

This is different from the Visualization techniques or the Play Pretend techniques, in that you are trying on different perspectives to see what you like, and to learn more about varying positions and roles. This *Flip the Hat* technique is much like trying on different hats, in order to see which one(s) you like best.

You *Flip the Hat* by:

> 1). Gathering as much information as you can about the position or role.

2). Put yourself in the places and environments where this position is functioning and functioning well.

3). Talk to the people who are already working in those positions and glean their particular views on the role.

4). Become aware of your *state of being* in connection with the role.

5). Decide if the role is for you based on your *state of being* rather than logic alone.

The first three steps could all be summed up as gathering data. The information that you obtain from getting data from third party sources like videos, books, the internet, etc., is essential to getting an overall idea of what the position is all about. It will give you a general overview.

After this you would want to go where this role is being per-formed, so you can see the role in action. For example, going to a company and sitting in on meetings and so on in order to witness a CEO in action. You watching videos and reading are great, but there is no substitute for actually being there. Being there will allow you to come into first hand contact with the energy of that position; and you can see and *feel* its impact on the environment. Books and videos will not give you this experience. Then you would want to meet the people who work in those positions. Doing this, will give you an inside track on what doing the position is like.

I realize that some may think actually doing the position would also give you real insight, and it would. But keep in mind the nature of this technique. *Flipping the Hat* is a process that is done lightly. That is, you want to be able to 'feel -out' if you want to take on a position or role, without actually going through all the processes of taking on that role. Getting in the actual place of being in that role, could take too long; and when you got there, you may discover that it's not right for you.

So after you collect all of this information, in these different ways, you want to make note of your *state of being*. That is your thoughts, emotions and physical body state. The *state of being* will intuitively, tell you what you need to know. Remember:

State of Being is the <u>experience</u> of a Perspective.

After being involved with all of this information about the position, that is, you watched videos, read books, been to the place where the position is happening, talked to the people who are doing it, etc. After all of this, you will have developed a perspective...for sure. Now to know if this position is something you want to pursue, you let your true thoughts, feelings and body states come through on that position or role. At this point, it's about you being honest with yourself about how you think and feel. Your state of being will not lie to you. All of this you can know and decide upon in a matter of seconds; and then flip your hat on to something else.

The core of this technique is about you being honest with yourself. Often times we want to please family and friends; or impress coworkers by doing things that are not true to who we really are. This is a great technique because it gives you a chance to see what being in a certain position would be like, without taking all of the time, which could be years, of getting into that position. You gain perspective, and experience this perspective as your *state of being*. Your logical mind, on the other hand, can be cajoled and finessed into a million different contortions. We can lie and fool ourselves with our 'logic'; and many times we can think too much and miss the mark on living authentically. However, your *state of being* will never lie; it just is what it is! By you being tuned into your *state of being,* it becomes just a matter of being honest about what you think and feel.

In this chapter, I have given you techniques that will cause a change in your perspective. Once you change your perspective, your life will change. In order to use these techniques, you don't have to dive deep and go into the silence of a meditative state. These techniques use the *Indirect Method* of choosing. And as such, are to be used in the context of your everyday life. That is, in the shower, in the car, on your lunch break, while you are interacting with your coworker, while you are cooking dinner, at the end of the day when you are listening to your significant other, and so on. Choose which technique fits you best at any given time... they are all powerful.

At the end of chapter three, I mentioned how the 3 Tools not only have the dual function that we discussed, but that they have a third aspect as well. The third aspect of the tools is their ability to create a change in Perspective by being turned inward and used as techniques in their own right. Let's return to this, in the next chapters...shall we.

Principles

1). Every significant break-through is the result of a change in Perspective.

2). Facing reality is the first step towards getting to where you want to be in life.

3).These techniques are based on the Indirect Method of choosing your perspective.

4). These Techniques must be done with understanding **and** feeling in the emotions and physical body. Logic alone will not create real change.

5). **Express Gratitude** is a Technique that brings the light of con-sciousness into all aspects of the self; and is a form of confron-tation.

6). The **Visualize Technique** uses inner vision to shape and cre-ate.

7). **Pre-Paving** uses the **Visualize Technique** to envision how you want things to unfold during the course of the day. You are also feeling in your emotions and physical body how the things *feel* that you want to happen.

8). When you **Visualize the Big Picture**, you are envisioning a larger goal. You are using your state of being to help you to choose the best perspective.

9). With the **Play Pretend-for real Technique**, you live out in the outer world what you want to be….before you become it.

10). The **Swap and Walk Technique**: this technique is about un-derstanding the perspective of another. You *Swap* places with someone else and you *Walk* in their shoes for a change.

11). The **Flip the Hat Technique** is a process where you take on the perspective of a position or role that you want to play or learn more about. This is not about understanding a person, but it's about understanding a perspective that goes with a role or position (for example, a manager. doctor, teacher, housewife, etc.) that you are curious in learning more about, or that you think you might want to take on.

Nathan Wallace

Chapter 6

Extended Techniques- *Thought*

Thought, word and action are the 3 Tools that we use to manifest our perspectives into the outer world. These tools also manifest for us by drawing back to themselves people, events, situations and things. What we will cover in this chapter is how these tools can be a great way to shift and create perspectives by turning them inward. There is unlimited potential in realizing the power that dwells in what you think, say and do. With an appreciation of their power, thought, word and action can be amazing techniques of change in their own right.

<u>Thought</u>

Thought can be used to radically transform who we are. It has been said that you are what you think. Once again, this is ancient wisdom. What we are going to do is look at a couple of techniques, which use our thought to shift and change our perspective(s).

A). Inner Mosaic Craft

Many mosaics are crafted from several pieces of beautiful glass. These small pieces of glass are usually of different sizes and shapes. All of these different pieces of colored glass are placed together to form a complete, beautiful image. This image is often transparent, allowing all of the different colors and sizes of the glass to reflect and disperse light. The mosaic allows the light to pass through the beautiful, multicolored glass and come into view.

This *Inner Mosaic Craft* technique is based on what a mosaic is, what we experience from it, and how it's made. Think of your perspective as the fully created mosaic...it is beautiful and unified, creating its own unique and beautiful view, casting its own light. The individual pieces of colored glass are your different thoughts. Each thought is of a different size, shape and color that all fit together to create the wonderful perspective-mosaic.

You are the artist here. You have an idea of what you want the mosaic to look like, and you carefully, with feeling and under-standing, collect the different pieces of colored glass to com-pose the complete mosaic.

We collect thoughts, like pieces of colored glass, around an idea of seeing things that would serve us best.

What we are doing with this is selecting thoughts based on what perspective we want to have. The perspective(s) we want to have is again, determined by us based upon how we want our lives to be like; based on what we want to be, do and have. We collect thoughts, like pieces of colored glass, around an idea of seeing things that would serve us best. We collect the thoughts over time and allow them to unify and strengthen one another until our attitude about a given subject has totally changed, and a new attitude (mosaic) has formed. The thoughts unify, strengthen and eventually form our new perspective. This happens by us *using the new thoughts that we have selected, instead of the old thoughts that belong to the perspective that we want to change.* We use these new thoughts with feeling. This is a cumulative process, that eventually causes a shift in our view; and therefore how we experience life in relation to the given perspective.

Let's say I have a fear of public speaking. I've tried speaking in public a few times and it turned out disastrous! I forgot and mispronounced the words, my voice and hands were shaking and I even froze up. This is not the *state of being* that I want to be in. I see other people having a good time and speaking in public effortlessly...and I want to do that. Now, I understand that any *state of being* comes out of a perspective. My state of being when I speak in public, let's me know that the inner perspective that I have, that relates somehow to public speaking, is out of harmony with it. In other words at some level, I am holding attitudes, beliefs and mental views that go against and do not serve my desire to do public speaking.

At this point, I could try and search within myself to find out what this limiting perspective is; and that would be a perfectly valid approach. That approach would be along the lines of the *Direct Method* that we discussed earlier in the book. So I could use some sort of practice or activity that would bring forth Mindfulness within me, and in that place, I would become aware of what those limiting views and attitudes were. From there I could make a different choice.

However, as I mentioned earlier, we are focusing on the *Indirect Method* of choosing a new perspective. Using this way, I choose thoughts that match up with me speaking in public effectively. These thoughts can come from various places...videos, books, conversations, different experiences, etc.

As long as the thoughts serve me and work together to make a perspective that allows me to be a good public speaker.

Choose over and over again, the new thoughts that serve you.

This is the key to forming your new perspective out of the thoughts you have gathered. There will be a tendency to think the way you used to think. But those old thoughts will only produce that same old perspective. So what you do is consciously choose (with feeling) to think the thoughts that you want, the thoughts that you have deliberately chosen. Thoughts that you know will serve you.

So in the public speaking example given above, I watch videos, read books, talk to friends, go to seminars, etc. In the process of doing all of this, I will have collected many powerful ideas on how to speak in public effectively. These ideas that I have collected, will contradict those old, ineffective ideas I had; ideas that did not help me to be able to speak in public well. Now, just because of sheer habit, I will have a tendency to go to those old ideas first...but I will stop myself. When public speaking comes up, I will consciously and deliberately choose to think the new thoughts! This is where my power is!

So:

1). You must have a clear idea of what you want to be, do and have.

2). Then you gather powerful thoughts that align with the outlook that best serves what you want.

3). You build the new perspective by thinking the new thoughts (with feeling) that you have gathered. You choose to think these new thoughts on the given subject... *instead of* the old, useless or random thoughts that belong to a vague or unwanted perspective.

4). Continue to think *over and over again* with the new powerful thoughts you have gathered. This will eventually become the way you think and thus your mental view on the given subject.

This is how you deliberately choose your perspective, and thus your life, with this Inner Mosaic Technique. Realize, that when you deliberately move your mind to the new thoughts that you have chosen, it may feel weird. You are not used to thinking in this new way, that's only natural. But understand **you** are determining your life...not your thoughts! By knowing what you want to be, do and have, you will know what serves you. When you deliberately choose the thoughts that will form a desired perspective, **and think them on purpose, with feeling in your emotional and physical body**...you will have the life that you want! You will become the driver of your life. Not vague, imprinted thoughts that hold you back...that you did not choose! You will become the conscious master of your life!

B). Focus Molding

Whatever you focus on grows. In this technique, we deliberately use this idea to mold for ourselves a new perspective. You will start from knowing what you want to be, do and have. Then you will pay attention to the people, places, things, ideas, feelings, etc., that *mold within you* a perspective that is like whatever you are paying attention to. This of course, is the *Indirect Method* of choosing your perspective, and thus your life.

This is a very deliberate and focused way to choose your perspective(s) that is mobile. That is, you can practice this technique, deliberately anytime you are awake.

When you pay attention and give your focus to something, eventually you will begin to incorporate that into your energy and pick up its vibe. When you pick up its vibe, you will eventually become like it. Have you ever heard of the phrase 'birds of a feather flock together'? This catchy little phrase contains a ton of deep wisdom. Ever heard 'you shall know a tree, by its fruit'? This is another revealing phrase that is of ancient and powerful wisdom. When someone really gets the revelation of this truth, many things about life, and themselves, become clear. You realize how, whatever you are paying attention to, slowly gets included in your being-ness, and you start to match up with it.

To be able to create your life just by what you pay attention to, is a wonderful attribute!

This is an innate, gift that we have that comes from The Creator. To be able to create your life just by what you pay attention to, is a wonderful attribute! However, this can be a huge source of miscreation for those who are not aware. The reason for this miscreation is that when you are giving your attention to what you don't want, you are opening the doorway to that unwanted stuff to come into your life. Now when I say 'pay attention', I mean putting any aspect of your awareness on something. This could be looking at it, listening to it, or putting any of the other five senses to it. Also using your mind to ponder or contemplate it; or allowing your feelings to dwell on it. I can't stress enough how powerful of an ability this is that we all possess!

For example, if you've ever had friends that did things that you knew were no good for you, what did you do? You got away from them. You stopped entertaining their ideas and thoughts; and in place of being with them, you did something constructive with yourself. This is using this ability in the right way. But what we want to do is turn this into a technique of deliberate creation. That is, it becomes something you do on purpose to get a desired result, time after time. I want you to realize, that you have this innate ability working all the time, anyway. So what we want is to take it from a semi-conscious, vague and random-like thing; and begin to direct it towards what we want so that it can perform in our lives the way it was designed to. To use it to transform and accomplish, is to use it proactively; rather than using it to get out of unwanted situations or to block out and avoid things. It is naturally a powerful creative tool that just takes our **intention** to direct it towards the things that we want to become like, experience and draw to us.

You must use your intention to place your attention on what you want to grow.

Your intention is what transforms the unconscious and pointless use of your attention, into a powerfully directed creative tool. A tool that you can use with very little physical action-effort, that will create a whole world around you. It does this by creating Perspective. When you deliberately and consciously pay attention to things because you understand the power of doing so, you are now being the conscious creator. You are molding within yourself, perspectives that serve you. This is, in effect, taking responsibility for your life.

Stop complaining. When you don't like someone, or you don't like what's going on or you are unhappy with your circumstances, *and* you are complaining about them, you are involved in miscreation. You are making all of that unwanted stuff bigger and bigger in your life. People often make at least two mistakes with this:

1). Talking about what they don't want to themselves (and everybody else) over and over again because they don't want it. I know it sounds circular...and it is! To feel like you need to talk constantly about what you don't want because you don't want it, and you have to be honest about the fact that you don't want it...will **not** create change. All you have done is talk about what you don't want and why you don't want it...so now what? You have gotten very clear on what you don't want, and so has everyone else that you have been complaining to. So now, as a result, what you don't want has gotten bigger in everyone's mind. But the solution, that is what you **do** want, has not. Not only has what you don't want gotten bigger in everyone's mind, but you've caused them, as well as yourself, to relive your emotional pain and discomfort as you were explaining it to them!

There is nothing wrong with being aware of what is not wanted, in fact it is all part of the 'getting- clear- about- what- we- want' process. *Once again, we must face reality. But to keep our focus on the unwanted and accept that as reality, will not create a solution for us*. We cannot create a better life this way. So instead of the solution getting clearer and energizing us, the problem just sits there and stagnates.

2). Believing that they need to focus on it in order to change it. This is something like '1).' above, but with an important difference. When someone feels like they need to focus on what they don't want, in order to fix it, they *are* using this technique with intention, but they are using it on the *wrong* stuff. This is in contrast to the person above who is just complaining and not trying to create a change on purpose. In this case, the idea that 'if I look at the unwanted situation over and over, deeper and deeper, I can make it better' is the <u>misapplication of intention</u>. Intention used to apply your focus to what you don't want, is still not focusing on solutions.

So if my car is giving me problems starting up, I can open the hood and look for the problem, or study it through videos, but that won't solve the issue. This just gets me clear on what the problem is. At some point I have to focus on *how* it can be solved. This seems obvious, right? But how many times has someone came to you with all of their problems? They weren't necessarily complaining about them, but the person knew all about them, how they came about and why they were happening. So with all of this knowledge, why were there still problems? The problems were still there with this person because they have used their intention to focus their thoughts and words on the problem...not on *how* they can change the problem.

Feeling <u>moves</u> you into the reality of what you are focusing on.

So now that you understand all of this, will putting up pictures of 'in shape' people all over your house cause you to lose that excess weight on your body and get 'in shape'? After all, you are focusing on what you want. You see the pictures when you get up in the morning, as you get dressed, when you come home at night, etc.

Using your intention to place your attention on what you want is a key ingredient, but this alone is incomplete. You need to *feel*. Feeling <u>moves</u> you into the reality of what you are focusing on. A very important feeling to let radiate is the feeling of **Positive Expectancy**, as was discussed earlier in this book. So when you do this *Focus Molding Technique*, you aren't just looking at pictures of what you want, or talking about what you want or thinking about it. **You are putting some feeling into it and at the same time, letting yourself feel how good it will feel to be, do or have what you want.** You allow yourself to feel this in your emotions and in you physical body. Experiencing this Positive Expectancy will *move* you to taking action. You will not have to 'push' yourself to do things. You will start doing stuff to get to where you want to be, with focus, clarity and a very joyful invincibility! Nothing will be able to get you down. By focusing this way emotionally, mentally and physically, you will snowball into what you desire.

So using the above example, when you look at the pictures of the people that are 'in shape', don't just look. You need to imagine how good you would feel being 'in shape'. You actually feel that good emotion in yourself, in the Now...in the present moment, even before you actually arrive at being 'in shape'. Feel it in your emotions as excitement, confidence, etc. Also imagine how your body would feel... your body would feel stronger, tighter, etc. All of this will spur you to change the current reality you have of not being 'in shape'. You will start using these techniques to move into your new reality with a passion that magnifies and is relentless!

Principles

1). *The 3 Tools* can be a great way to shift and create perspectives by turning them inward.

2). ***Inner Mosaic Craft Technique*** is based on what a mosaic is, what we experience from it, and how it's made. We collect thoughts, like pieces of colored glass, around an idea of seeing things that would serve us best. We collect the thoughts over time and allow them to unify and strengthen one another until our attitude about a given subject has totally changed, and a new attitude (mosaic) has formed. Thoughts and ideas are strengthened by using them with feeling.

3). **Focus Molding Technique:** *whatever you focus on grows. In this technique,* you pay attention to the people, places, things, ideas, feelings, etc., that *mold within you* a perspective that is <u>like</u> whatever you are paying attention to. This technique uses **Intention** in its process. Your intention is what transforms the unconscious and pointless use of your attention, into a powerfully directed creative tool.

4). With the *Focus Molding Technique,* you are putting some feeling into it and at the same time, letting yourself feel how good it will feel to be, do or have what you want. We know this as **Positive Expectancy**; and it is involved with all techniques of change more or less.

Chapter 7

Extended Techniques-*Word*

The second of the 3 Tools that we will look at, as a technique of change, is Word. As I mentioned in a previous chapter, words are a very powerful tool for change. The conscious use of words to create our inner perspective or to call what we want to be, do and have into existence is us choosing the life we want. Below are some techniques for using this power.

Word

A). I Am Maker

This is what I call the I Am Maker Technique. With this technique, you are turning your words inward, towards the self, and creating your *state of being*. The definition of *State of Being* was covered in an earlier chapter; please feel free to review this, if necessary. When you use words to determine your state of being, you have shifted your perspective. Once you have shifted your perspective, your life will change. The object of this technique is to choose words that will create the life experience that you want to have.

You are using the power of words on yourself.

I Am is the key in using this technique in order to create. I Am is to be put before the word that you will use. For example, *I Am* great; *I Am* strong; *I Am* blessed, and so on. Using I Am before the descriptive word automatically turns this tool inward. What you are doing here is using the power of words on yourself. **You are claiming who you are and you are affecting your state of being.**

Remember that words have an inherent power of their own, just by virtue of the word being used. So when you say 'I am well', just the statement itself carries a definitional meaning for you. In other words, the definition of the word 'well' carries its own meaning as 'something good'. That much is obvious, *but there is power itself in the definition of a word.*

Secondly, remember that words have energy placed into them by the speaker. This is what we called the 'vibe' of the word. So when I say 'I am well', I can say this with a feeling of confidence and enthusiasm, or I can say it with doubt and lethargy. When you say 'I am well' (according to its desired meaning) with good emotions, it will have a more potent and faster effect on your state of being than if you were to say it with doubtful, unenthusiastic emotion.

...this technique is declaring who and what you are and claiming your inner state of being...

What you are doing with this technique is declaring who and what you are and claiming your inner state of being, which in turn determines your perspective and thus your life. This is a powerful technique for personal transformation that can be done anywhere. Once you know what you want to experience, you speak to yourself or to others along the lines of the desired experience. So, for example, if you want to be financially prosperous, say 'I am blessed'. Not 'I am broke'. Even if you have no money in your pocket, still say 'I am blessed'. You say this until you feel it more and more, and until you begin to truly believe it. Your *'state of being'* will change...meaning you will begin to feel prosperous and have prosperous thoughts. This in turn means that your perspective has changed from "I am broke and a loser" to "I am prosperous and blessed".

Now this is the point at which some people will break away and disagree with me. The argument goes something like this: "I understand what you're saying about using my words and all, but it feels like a lie when I say something that I know is **not** true. So you want me to say that I'm prosperous when I know I don't have any money...that's not true, and I feel fake, like a liar when I say it. It's just not reality".

We are concerned with creating what we want, not with what's already true.

When we are using this technique, we are not interested in speaking what is; we are interested in speaking into being what we *want* to experience. When a painter comes to a blank canvas to paint a picture, the canvas is white, it's blank, and there is nothing on it. The fact that the canvas is blank *is* the truth. But the painter doesn't stop there; if they did, the work of art would never be produced. As far as the 'reality' of the situation being that there is no money in the bank account, we know this, but that won't stop us from doing what we can to change it. Listen*: learn to disregard a reality that does not serve you, and create one that does.*

In this technique, you speak your 'I Am' truth no matter what the circumstances may be or look like at that moment. This is your power as a creator, as the artist of your life. This is not being 'fake', lying or in denial of current reality. What you are doing is taking dominion over your reality, this is your responsibility! So the next time someone asks you how you are, tell them you are great. In the reality of that moment, you may feel great or you may not, it doesn't matter. **This is not about feelings or what's 'true'. This is about us knowing the power of our words to create, and then exercising that power!**

B). Arise

This technique is a bit different than the others, in that this one works on the outer world more so than our inner world. The Arise Technique is about us using our words to bring forth. This is about us bringing forth in the outer world what will cause a shift in our inner state *of being*. Which in turn means that our perspective has shifted; and that ultimately means that we have chosen a new life experience. This 'bringing forth' is not done with action, but with words.

We must use the power that this technique has, by speaking along the lines of what we want to be, do and have. This is just like the I Am Maker Technique in that we are deliberately speaking into being what we desire. *So it's not about conforming our words to what is apparently 'true' in the outer world; we can obviously see what the reality is. We are using our power to speak into being and bring forth a new truth, one that serves us.*

Perspective gives rise to reality.

Everything that you see ultimately comes from what you cannot see. Mind gives rise to matter. Perspective gives rise to reality. At this very moment, I am writing this book and soon you will find it on your device or in your hands. This book exists within me; I then feel it and get the idea of what to say. I then pass that idea through my fingers, and then I tap the keys on the keyboard. The words then appear on the screen in front of me... the book is now in physical reality. Do you see how the process works? This book is coming from an invisible place, within me, into a physical manifestation that your senses can pick up. This book has gone from the invisible to the visible.

Furthermore, I am only writing this book because of my perspective. That is, if I had a different perspective, I would never even write the book! Let me explain. To sit down and take the time to write this, I need to have an attitude of faith. I need to believe that doing all of this will help someone; that it's worthwhile because of that. So the perspective I have is that I am doing something that will help other people to live a fuller, more joyful and empowered life. If I didn't see it this way, I would not put in all of the time it took to write this book and get it into your hands. So you see how my perspective on writing this book, has made it not only a reality within itself, but my perspective has made it a reality that is now in your hands? That is the power of perspective in a nutshell.

So how does this relate to the Arise Technique? *The fact that Perspective gives rise to reality means that by using your words to call forth a perspective, you are calling forth the life, the reality that you want to experience.* So for example, let's say that it's 90 degrees outside, so it's pretty hot. I and a friend are trying to decide on how we can enjoy the day. My friend says: "it is 90 degrees outside; it's too hot to go out. So I think I'll stay inside, under the air conditioner, and watch a movie". I on the other hand, say: "ok it is 90 degrees outside; that's perfect. So I think I'll ride my bike and maybe stop at the beach and go for a swim".

There are two different perspectives going on here about the temperature of the weather. My friend sees it as being 'too hot', but I see it as 'perfect'. So based on this, we end up having two different sets of experiences on that day. Keep in mind that we are dealing with the same outer reality, that is, 90 degree weather. But because we spoke of it differently, we each brought forth...*made arise*, two different life experiences. We could both say that it is 90 degrees outside, but that would just be data, facts. Remember as human beings we are thinking, feeling beings that create. So the fact that it's a certain temperature outside is just what we perceived with our senses. We are also going to have an attitude or mental view (perspective) that we impress upon the 'raw' data. So my perspective about what I perceive is spoken..."it is 90 degrees outside; that's perfect". Once I have spoken it, my reality now continues to match up with what I have spoken.

You are making worlds arise from within yourself, just from the words that you use!

When you are dealing with people, situations, places, things etc., which are in the outer world, speak about them in the way you want them to be. This means speaking them *into* the way of being that best serves your highest aspirations for yourself and everyone involved. For example, say there is a discussion on your job, you could see the people as being silly, ignorant and barbaric. Or you could see these people as intelligent with some real important concerns that they are voicing. There's always what we perceive, then the *mental view* that we *impress* on the 'raw' perception. This was explained in chapter one. When we impress our views on something that we are experiencing, a whole universe of other thoughts, words, actions, feelings and perceptions are set in motion. This 'universe' will correspond with the perception...creating a life experience or reality.

The point of the Arise technique is for you to *consciously* set in motion the gears of this creation machine. It then becomes not a matter of just saying what you see; but it becomes a matter of speaking what you want your life to be like… in relation to whatever you perceive. So using the above example, if you want to create within yourself a good emotion about the 'discussion' on your job, you would use your words to describe it in matching terms. So you would say stuff like…'they're working out some issues' or 'it's great that they are being honest with each other and resolving some things'. These words offer up a perspective that leads to positive emotion within you. This positive emotion is part of what makes up your state of being. From this place, your 3 Tools get to work on translating the perspective further outward into 3-D reality and at the same time drawing back to you what is like them; and so on and so on it goes. So here (in this example) you can see that while I was speaking of an outer event, I deliberately used words to create a change **within** myself. You are making worlds arise from within yourself, just from the words that you use!

Words are a powerful tool that you can consciously use to create perspective within yourself and thus, choose the life you want. What I've seen, is that people tend to regard action as the main way to get their lives the way they want. Without a doubt, action is an amazing way to create within yourself and the outside world. However, also give serious consideration to the words that come from you…as these are equally as powerful.

Principles

1). The *I Am Maker Technique*. With this technique, you are turning your words inward (towards the self) by using the power of the words I AM _____. You are deliberately using the words I AM _____, to claim and declare who you are; thus creating your *state of being* and your life.

2). When we are using the *I Am Maker Technique*, we are not interested in speaking what is; we are interested in speaking into being what we *want* to experience.

3). *Learn to disregard a reality that does not serve you, and create one that does.*

4). The **Arise Technique** is about us using our words to bring forth. This is about us bringing forth in the outer world what will cause a shift in our inner *state of being, and thus our lives.*

5). The *Arise Technique* is *not* about conforming our words to what is apparently 'true' in the <u>outer world</u>; we can obviously see what the reality is. We are using our power to speak into being and bring forth a *new truth*, one that serves us.

6). Perspective gives rise to reality.

Nathan Wallace

Chapter 8

Extended Techniques-*Action*

The last of the 3 Tools that we will visit is Action. By Action, we mean *physical interaction* with the outer, physical world. Action, just like Thought and Word, can be turned inward and used as a way to deliberately create Perspective within us. As we have seen, all of the tools are equally powerful to use in choosing and living the life we desire; a life that is a gift and the greatest version of ourselves that we can imagine.

Action

A). Self-Move

The Self-Move Technique is done by using action *with the self* to cause a change in perspective. You are using action <u>with yourself</u> to create a shift in your *state of being* (thus your perspective). This, like all of the techniques, is done deliberately. This technique is used with the conscious intent to create a state of being that matches up with the state of being that goes with what you want. So if, for example, people who are satisfied in their relationships are manifesting *peacefulness*, then you would *do actions* with yourself that would create this state of *peacefulness* within you. So you might go to a pond or lake and relax, look at the birds and so on. This would produce that state of inner peacefulness within you. You would then go back to your personal relationship(s) with this peacefulness, and have a different experience, a different reality within that relationship.

So, as always, you start from an awareness of what you want to be, do and have. You then allow yourself to become aware of what state of being you are currently in. You may be currently excited, fearful, courageous, and with thoughts and body states to match. Let's say you notice that people with their own businesses have a lot of energy, and always think optimistically. Currently, however you are working a 9 to 5 job and it seems like you have just enough energy to go back and forth to work every day. Also, you don't have a negative mindset, but at the same time, you don't think as optimistically as the business owners do either.

This is where the Self-Move Technique can help out. You are doing stuff to change your state of being. Because when that has changed, you know your perspective has changed, thus giving you a new, matching life experience to what you want. So in this case, you could do something that would work with the physical aspect of your state of being. You could start exercising to get your energy levels up. You could also start to give consideration to what you eat. Is the food you eat now healthy? What types of foods do you eat? How often do you eat? Then look at your sleep patterns, do you get enough sleep at night? Do you feel rested when you wake up in the morning?

These are considerations relative to what you have decided you want. Remember that you came to the conclusion that you want your own business. You then became aware that people who had their own businesses had a lot of energy and were optimistic. These two characteristics you felt that you didn't have at the same level. So you deliberately started moving your state of being to a place where you have comparable energy and optimism as the business owners. So you then start dealing with your current state of being... you begin working out, you eat different foods and you get the rest that you need.

...change the self before trying to do something in the outer world.

Using this Self-Move Technique is the best way to use action to move into something new. It's always best to look at the self and to change the self before trying to do something in the outer world. This is the reason why, so often, people give up and fail at their aspirations. Many have not moved their state of being into a harmonious place *before* jumping into action on some endeavor. As a result, they are unprepared...on the inside, at the level of self. The amazing thing about effecting a change in self, is that once you make a real, solid impact on one aspect of your state of being, the other aspects will gravitate in that same direction.

So, from the example above, you started exercising your body, this in itself will start the momentum in your favor. Remember that we said *State of Being* is made up of the thoughts, emotions and physical body-states. So by exercising, you are moving the body-state aspect into a new place. This will create more health, vitality and immediate energy in your body, which in turn will help you to sleep better. With these changes, ideas and feelings will come that you could only experience with this new level of energy and vitality, because they match up with it. This surge in a higher level of thinking can appear unexpectedly. But when you raise your body-state energy levels and vitality, your thought levels will automatically get higher as well. **Remember that the thoughts, emotions and body-states that compose your state of being, are drawing to themselves more *'like' thoughts, emotions and body states.*** What you are doing is using this principle, to make changing your perspective easier and faster.

This Technique can be used in such a simple way as doing some push-ups or jumping jacks to get the 'blood flowing' before going into a meeting, for example. Now, it should be clear about what's going on: doing the jumping jacks is having a direct impact on the body-state aspect of our state of being. So once this aspect has been stimulated, our thoughts and emotions will pick up as well. All of this better prepares us for the meeting.

The elegance of this technique is that it can be applied in even more simple, immediate ways. Say, for example, something irritates you, which makes you feel not so good. You *do* have the choice to sit in that irritation, or not. A quick way to begin moving yourself out of this state of being is to *smile*. What you are doing when you smile, is deliberately creating with yourself and with your body, an expression that matches up with the state that you want to be in, which is a pleasant one. This simple act that you are doing with your self will begin the movement of your entire state of being and thus your perspective in the direction you want. Once again, we don't care about this smile looking fake; and we don't even care if the smile feels fake. Yes, we know that we are irritated...so what! It's not about the 'truth'. It's about the reality that we want to experience. It's about choosing the life we want to live... a life lived in the most magnificent way that we can imagine!

B). Engage Shift

The Engage Shift Technique is performed by engaging with the <u>outer world</u> through *action*, in order to shift your state of being. By now, we know this causes a change in Perspective, which causes a change in one's life experience, i.e., reality. Another way to say that is, you do things in the outer world in order to change how you think and feel.

The actions that you do with this technique are all done with the intention of creating a shift within yourself. This is different from the Self-Move Technique in that this Engage Shift Technique is about you doing stuff in the *outer world* to change your perspective. Whereas with the Self-Move Technique, you are doing things *with yourself* in order to change your perspective.

The actions that you do are done with honesty and sincerity.

The actions that you do are done with honesty and sincerity. That means you are not doing actions that are fake and manipulative. However, the actions that you do with this technique *are* done selfishly. Now be aware that to act out of 'selfishness' is not necessarily a bad or evil thing. In fact, we all act selfishly all the time. What I mean by this is that everyone can only act from the self, and out of the self. This includes a person's strengths and weaknesses, their cultural background and environment, and also their perception and perspectives. So acting selfishly, is unavoidable. What we usually mean is that someone who acts selfishly is acting without regards for another and only with regards for the self; often at the expense of another in a negative way. Well, that type of action is not the aim of this book. To act selfishly, in our context, means that you are aware of a larger concept of how your actions create ripple effects within *yourself*. These 'ripple effects' that are created in you, within your state of being, make up your perspective(s). Now your perspectives govern how you think, speak and act in the outer world. So then, these thoughts, words and actions that you are doing *are* affecting the earth, people, animals, etc. Here, with this technique, you are doing things in the outer world that are sincere within their own right. The things that you do are also 'designed' to create a perspective within you, which uplifts yourself; and thus the outer world that we all live in.

As an example, a few years ago I wanted to increase my finances and lifestyle. After some self-examination, I realized that my perspective on money was preventing me from growing financially. I was valuing money too much. I would try and hold on to as much money as I could, out of the fear of losing it. So I lived beneath my means, I would buy cheaper stuff (that wouldn't last), and so on. Living this way was no fun; and what I came to realize is that I had limiting beliefs that amounted to fear around the subject of money.

So I realized the solution was to begin to *not* care so much about money...to stop clutching onto every dime for dear life. The way I helped myself, was to start giving it away. I always would see many homeless people on the street begging for money. In the past, I would give every now and then; but now I decided to give money to them on a regular basis. So from 3 to 5 days a week, I would give to the homeless people on the street. When I gave, I sincerely wanted them to have the money. I also knew that it was helping me to let go of my fears concerning money.

After a while, I noticed that I began to feel different about money. I began to lose my fear of not having it. I also noticed that I began to feel more prosperous within myself. Then two other things happened: One, I began to have more money! At the time, I didn't have as complete of a picture as I do now, about how this Perspective stuff works. But it was a great feeling to experience helping someone else and then having those same blessings come back to me!

Secondly, I got an idea to start a Not-for-Profit organization to help displaced and struggling creative people. I know now that it was due to my improved inner *state of being* that I was even able to have that kind of idea, genuinely within myself. **The improved perspective that I had acquired, gave me the state of being that could produce that kind of idea.** This is a real-life example, which demonstrates this Engage Shift Technique, very clearly.

"How can I grow and be more of a gift to the world"?

So as always, you start off knowing what you want to be, do and have. From this knowing, ask yourself with respect to a given subject: "how can I grow and be more of a gift to the world"? This type of question is the best way to enter into this technique; because with this type of question, you are setting up the inflow and outflow of energy. Meaning that by asking… 'How can I grow?' you are putting forth the desire for inner change. Then by asking '…and be more of a gift to the world?' you are putting forth the desire to bring goodness into the outer world. The answer you receive will answer both parts of the question. The circle will be complete.

From this stance, you now act on what you know. So if the answer you get is to do volunteer work at the zoo, then you go do that. When you go about doing what you need to do, it must be done authentically and with a sincere, good heart. *You must take sincere joy in seeing your actions benefit who or whatever you are helping in the outside world.* If however, you are doing these things just to get a benefit for yourself, all of the actions that you take will not benefit you. You must surrender to the action and do it for its own sake, doing it unconditionally… in spite of you knowing how the bigger picture works. So if you are doing volunteer work at the zoo, for example, *genuinely care* about the animals! Love them and do whatever you can to help them be well and happy; and leave it right there. The blessings of doing this were foreseen by you, but when you are doing it, you are doing it from your heart! All you have to do is be open and the blessings and benefits of your actions will soon rain down on you like a hurricane!

So a general approach to this technique would be:

1). Become clear on what you want to be, do and have.

2). Ask a question that will **create a circuit of energy**. Such as, "How can I grow and be more of a gift to the world"?

3). Take massive action.

4). When taking action, do the action with *unconditional sincerity*. That is, without regards to any outcome for yourself.

5). *Allow* the many blessings and benefits to come to you in their own time and in their own way.

The Engage Shift Technique will create a positive and powerful flow of goodness from you to the world and the world back to you. This is the meaning of living a life of Love, prosperity and power. This is also living your truth. To be able to take action, and do things to better the world and ourselves, is one of the greatest gift we have.

Principles

1). The **Self-Move Technique** uses action with the self to cause a change in perspective.

2). It's always best to look at the self and to change the self before trying to do something in the outer world.

3). The **Engage Shift Technique** is performed by engaging with the outer world through *action*, in order to shift your state of being.

4). The actions that you do are done with honesty and sincerity. That means you are not doing actions that are fake and manipulative.

5). You are not overly invested in the reality that is...you are doing things in the outer world that will bring forth the reality you want.

6). You enter into this *Engage Shift Technique* by asking a question that sets up a *circuit of energy* that benefits you and the outer world.

Conclusion

No matter what you do or where you go, you will always have Perspective. This is a truth that we cannot escape; a truth that is a wonderful gift. To become the conscious chooser of your perspectives is to become the author of your life's story; and to live *your* truth. You don't have to be anything less than the magnificent soul that you are.

The ideas and techniques in this book will be an anchor for you. Use this book and refer to it frequently. This book's principles, concepts and techniques will never go out of style...they are timeless. A Mind for Life will help you to develop and experience the life that you always knew you were meant to live.

This is your time, go forth and create your life.

Nathan Wallace

<u>NOTES</u>

<u>NOTES</u>

<u>NOTES</u>

<u>NOTES</u>

<u>NOTES</u>